THE LAUGHING CLASSROOM

Other Books by Diane Loomans

Full Esteem Ahead:
100 Ways to Build Self-Esteem in Children and Adults

For Children

The Lovables in the Kingdom of Self-Esteem

The Lovables
(a board book for young children)

Positively Mother Goose
(coauthors, Karen Kolberg and Julia Loomans)

For Pre-teens

Today I am Lovable:
365 Positive Activities for Kids

THE LAUGHING CLASSROOM

Everyone's Guide
to Teaching With Humor and Play

Diane Loomans
Karen J. Kolberg

With a Foreword by Steve Allen
and a Backword by Professor Oops!

Illustrated by Martha Weston

H J KRAMER INC
Tiburon, California

H J Kramer Inc
P.O. Box 1082
Tiburon, CA 94920

Library of Congress Cataloging-in-Publication Data

Loomans, Diane, 1955–
   The laughing classroom : everyone's guide to teaching with humor
and play / Diane Loomans, Karen J. Kolberg : illustrated by Martha
Weston : with a foreword by Steve Allen and a backword by Professor
Oops!
      p.   cm.
   Includes bibliographical references.
   ISBN 0–915811–44–8
   1. Teaching.   2. Humor in education.   3. Teacher-student
relationships.   4. Classroom management.   I. Kolberg, Karen, 1954–
II. Title.
LB1027.L623   1993
371.1′02′0207–dc20   92–23351
                                                                                  CIP

Editors: Roberta Vinck and Nancy Grimley Carleton
Composition: Classic Typography
Production: Schuettge and Carleton

Manufactured in the United States of America.
10 9 8 7 6 5 4

This book is dedicated to:

My wild and crazy family,
who think fast on their feet
and know how to have a good laugh.

Sky Schultz,
professional fool
and inspiring friend,
who takes laughter seriously
and approaches life
with a light heart.
D. L.

My loving parents,
who encouraged and supported me
on my playful path.

Matt Weinstein,
my humor mentor.

Constance Hawkins,
an extraordinary educator
who embodies the lighthearted
spirit of this book.
K. J. K.

Contents

Foreword by Steve Allen   **ix**
Preface   **xi**

Part One: Becoming a Laughing Teacher   **1**

  1. The Possible Parable   3
  2. Becoming a Laughing Teacher   5
  3. Pop Quiz   9
  4. Fifty Excuses for Not Laughing   12
  5. Four Humor Styles   13
  6. The High Fives of Humor   20
  7. The Laughing Classroom Oath   21
  8. Song: "The Laughter Rap"   22
  9. Humor Homework   23
10. Play Sheet   24
11. Notes for Myself   25

Part Two: Creating a Laughing Classroom   **27**

12. Paula Parrot and the Carrot   29
13. Creating a Laughing Classroom   32
14. The Laughing Classroom Quiz   34
15. Fast and Fun: Thirty Ideas   36
16. Twenty-five Ways to Go the Extra Smile   52
17. The ABCs of Fun   54
18. Thanks to You   55
19. Song: "The Twelve Days of Classes"   58
20. Humor Homework   61
21. Play Sheet   62
22. Notes for Myself   63

Part Three: Tons of Techniques   65

23. Warm-ups   67
24. Laughing Lessons   92
25. Play Breaks   122
26. Notes for Myself   147

Part Four: Teaching With Humor That Heals   149

27. The Tribal Tale   151
28. Teaching With Humor That Heals   153
29. The Up-Tightrope Test   155
30. Say It, Replay It!   157
31. Before and Laughter Scenarios   160
32. Fifty Ways to Say You Did Okay   172
33. Exceptional Excuses   173
34. Song: "Nifty Ways to Learn by Laughing"   174
35. Humor Homework   175
36. Play Sheet   176
37. Notes for Myself   177

Part Five: Using Laughter Forever After   179

38. Through the Laughing Glass   181
39. Using Laughter Forever After   183
40. Let's Get Quizzical: A Humor Questionnaire   185
41. Ask Ann Laffers!   190
42. Glossary and "Giggliography"   203
43. Lighten Up Your Lounge!   206
44. Classroom Checklist   207
45. Song: "The Rattle Hymn"   209
46. Humor Homework   210
47. Play Sheet   211
48. Notes for Myself   212

Bibliography   213
"Backword" by Professor Oops!
(aka Sky Schultz, Ph.D.)   217

Foreword

by Steve Allen

As I look back at the years of my formal education—sketchy as it was—I find that three teachers stand out in my recollection. What they all had in common was a good sense of humor. Whether they taught their subjects any better than their relatively humorless equivalents I don't really know, but their geniality and their general good nature simply set a social context within which I felt comfortable. By way of contrast, I remember one instructor—she taught Spanish—who, because she was a critical, sarcastic, and cold person, was able to teach me very little.

The Laughing Classroom is a humorist's happy hands-on book that shows how to avoid such mistakes. Because it entertains, educates, and celebrates, it's a delight to read. You'll find even greater delight in the results you'll get when you apply the authors' techniques for combining laughter and learning in the classroom.

Every teacher knows that education is both an art and a science. The *science* of education involves the teacher's head—organizing, juggling schedules, making administrative decisions, and designing curriculum. The *art* of education makes use of a teacher's heart—acting as a role model, caring about students, listening to parents, and advocating for quality education. A teacher who uses only the head is called a taskmaster and often makes learning unpleasant and unnecessarily difficult. A teacher who uses only the heart can quickly burn out for lack of refueling. Obviously both the head and the heart should be involved.

Combining their talents with those of a brilliant illustrator, the authors offer a cornucopia of helpful suggestions that call on both head and heart. They introduce three kinds of easy-to-follow techniques—Warm-ups, Laughing Lessons, and Play Breaks—as a wonderful guide to help you travel the playful path. They have created a breakthrough model of four humor styles that will help you clearly analyze the humor styles of you and the people in your life. They nudge you a bit, showing simple and fast ways to add humor and heart to your teaching day.

In any field, masters have a healthy sense of humor and believe their work is a joyous necessity, not merely "necessary." Masters have compassion, yet maintain an inner equilibrium; they intelligently apply what they intuitively understand. Masters are respected and remembered. *The Laughing Classroom* can inspire you to become a master teacher.

Preface

If you are a teacher, congratulations! This book is for you. It's a guide to help you reawaken your playful, spontaneous self, which may have gotten lost somewhere between correcting the papers and collecting the paycheck. It's a plea for play—an appeal for you to tap your funny bone—not just on weekends or during vacations, but during your teaching day, when you have the most influence and power.

These pages contain methods for creating a learning environment filled with trust, creativity, spontaneity, wonder, and joy. You'll find self-help tests, parables, songs, and other funny ideas intended to evoke laughter, play, and bonding in your classroom. These techniques are designed to be simple, fun, and organized so that you can use them *today*, without a practice run. Through trial and error, we have polished and developed these techniques; they have proved successful with thousands of teachers and students throughout the country.

Although many of the techniques can be used for a multitude of purposes, some work most effectively for building rapport, some enhance the learning process, and others are great energizers. Because of this, we've divided the exercises into three main categories: Warm-ups, Laughing Lessons, and Play Breaks. Adopt them as they are or adapt them to meet your specific needs. As you experiment, you'll find that rearranging and changing them is half the fun. *Remember, in creative play, there are no wrong answers; there are only possibilities.*

This book is the joint effort of two people: Diane, a writer, educational consultant, and national speaker; and Karen, a writer, educator, entertainer, and national speaker.

As a college teacher and adult educator, Diane often dressed up in character, used props, wore wigs, passed out crayons, played music, dimmed the lights, danced and sang, and did whatever it took to create a safe atmosphere where the creative genius within each student could flourish. This included incorporating humor whenever possible, such as two minutes of playful Warm-up exercises and three- to five-minute Play Breaks for every hour of instruction. When Diane presented seminars, she added other playful elements: whistles, bells, masks, puppets, slides, and group interaction. Creative expression became the hallmark of her presentations. The original idea for this book grew out of Diane's experience with a national workshop she created that provides hands-on humor techniques for teachers.

Meanwhile, Karen, who had written over forty comedic theater productions and had cofounded ComedySportz, a national competitive theater company, received her professional training and development certificate to complement her degree in education. She soon discovered that she couldn't take the entertainment out of her training, nor did she want to entertain without educating, and so she became an "enter-trainer." She uses her juggling, comedy, characters, and teaching skills during her speeches and presentations. As a consultant for Playfair, she has experienced the tremendous power that humor and play have for building community while presenting Playfair's popular college-orientation icebreaker.

During the last fifteen years, we have observed that techniques that include laughter and play encourage learning. Although learning always requires effort, we discovered that whenever we included humor, learning occurred without fear, struggle, or self-deprecation. We have designed our seminars and workshops with the "funny factor" in mind, using ourselves as a gauge. When the material is not interesting, absorbing, or fun for us, it's probably not interesting or fun for our students either.

In writing this book, we have made every effort to model what we teach. When we write, we take frequent Play Breaks. When our creativity is blocked, we find something to laugh about. We have used humor to over-come our dysfunctional patterns of behavior. We want results, not only for ourselves, but for the groups that we lead. Because our philosophy about teaching is similar, it was natural for us to combine our talents and knowledge and share what we've learned about learning and laughter.

The result is a cornucopia of time-tested ideas, reflecting the years of experience we've had creating playful, practical teaching tools. Many techniques are original; we have adapted others from a variety of creative sources for use in the classroom. Resources are listed in the back of the book. We encourage you to explore them in depth.

Many of the techniques we present improve learning and will bring measurable results, from a dramatic increase in attention span to an increased ability to comprehend and remember material with ease. You'll feel a safety net of caring spread as minds expand, hearts open, conversations heighten, and bonding takes its rightful place in education. This nurturing net can help any group resolve problems and differences.

If you've encouraged laughter in your classroom and are dedicated to bringing joy and fun into the learning process, this book will provide you with new ideas and new combinations. For those of you who are struggling to maintain your sanity despite the overwhelming odds, or feel that your work is hazardous to your health, this book is also for you. Our goal is to relieve your "jest" pains, reduce your "humor-rhoids," and give you renewed energy and support for your work.

We have taken a practical, playful, and reverent look at the power of laughter as it relates to the learning process. We hope to dispel any "myth-understandings" you might have about laughter in the learning process while gently guiding you to "laugh long and prosper"!

✳   ✳   ✳

The Laughing Classroom is the creative, playful result of many great minds. We offer our respect and appreciation to those who helped, directly or indirectly, with the creation of this book. We thank Hal and Linda Kramer, our publishers, for their ongoing support and enthusiasm and their willingness to go the extra mile. Martha Weston brought life to many concepts with her playful, imaginative artwork. We thank Roberta Vinck for her wonderful editing and invaluable feedback, and Nancy Grimley Carleton for her great dedication and excellent editing. Namaste to Uma Ergil of H J Kramer for her caring spirit and creative marketing ideas, and many laughs to Mick Laugs of H J Kramer for his silly, insightful support.

Our work has been influenced by some of the greatest "pioneers of play," including Steve Allen, Steve Allen, Jr., Norman Cousins, Raymond Moody, Annette Goodman, Matt Weinstein, Joel Goodman, Sky Schultz, Alan Klein, and many more brilliant players.

Diane would like to thank the following people who contributed with their unique gifts:

- My coauthor, Karen Kolberg, for spending unlimited time at all hours brainstorming, writing, and creating with me, and for her devoted hours on the word processor. Thanks for going the distance. We did it!
- Precious Julia Loomans, for her wild imagination and ongoing inspiration.
- Lovable Michael Taibi, for sharing his loving support and playful spirit again and again.
- Jim Fitzpatrick, for the countless moments of hilarious improvisation and silliness that have influenced my own sense of humor and playfulness. Thanks, Dad!
- The San Diego Master Mind Group—Ann Albrecht, Gloria Boileau, Dianne Gardner, and Pamela Truax—for their great enthusiasm, love, and support.

- Marshall Rosenberg, who aspires to laugh all of his laughter and cry all of his tears.
- Michael Marois, for his brilliant and sensitive photography work.

Karen would like to thank the following playful people for their contributions:

- My coauthor, Diane Loomans, for her generosity of spirit, her honesty, her pursuit of excellence, and her dedication to teaching others how to become Joy Masters.
- My Playfair family, for their unconditional support of my work and their ability to bring joy to the world through high-level play.
- My Moon Group—Julianna, Suzanne, Peggy, Connie, Sally, and Mary—for their playfulness, their open hearts, their willingness to listen, and their extraordinary vision for the world.
- My "men-tors" and brainstorming buddies—Sky Schultz, Phill Modjeski, Axel Anderson, Norman Schwartz, Mark Stamm, and Paul Fleischman—for their encouragement and brilliant feedback.
- My photographer, David Poulos, for his professionalism, his talent, and his cheerful disposition.

Finally, both of us salute the countless heroes of the everyday world who inspire and uplift others with their humor, lightheartedness, and laughter. Your timeless influence graces these pages.

Becoming a Laughing Teacher

Part One

1

The Possible Parable

And God said, "Let there be education."

And, lo, there was education; and teachers, students, classrooms, principals, roll calls, bulletin boards, staff meetings, report cards, parent-teacher conferences, lunch tickets, playground duty, government mandates, more staff meetings, drug busts, weapon checks, colds on the weekends, bouts of flu during every vacation, and a whole host of tedious tasks that had less to do with teaching and more to do with discipline, conflict resolution, and classroom management. And God finished by saying, "Let there be education so we don't have to endure run-on sentences."

And the teachers said, "Let there be some relief." And, lo, there was relief—and respite, aid, rescue, and glorious, glad tidings. This gift of help came packaged in a simple, sweet phrase so all who were listening could hear. And the words that were spoken, and the words that were heard were "HA HA." "HA HA?" the teachers responded. "That's it? HA HA? You mean, we don't get smaller classes, larger salaries, more planning time, longer vacation time, fewer staff meetings, unconditional love from our principals, or permission to be excused from playground duty? There must be some mistake; this has to be a bad joke with no punch line."

The Great HA HA resounded throughout the heavens for a trimester and then dissipated into the ethers. The teachers, puzzled about the meaning of such a silly phrase, concluded that the laughter was being directed at them for spending such long hours, for such little pay, with so little appreciation or recognition! These truthful tidings became unbearable for many. The despondent teachers distracted

3

themselves by erasing everyone else's blackboards. The frustrated teachers went back to school to get their business degrees. A few teachers retired early, and some simply disappeared and still haven't been accounted for.

Time continued to be marked by the beginning and ending of the school year. Throughout the centuries, teachers began to slowly unravel the mysterious message of HA HA given to them so that they could be of greater service to their students.

You now hold a book that contains the teachings about the meaning of the Great HA HA, the when, where, why, and how of HA HA as it relates to your life and the life of your classroom. As the ancient wisdom was passed down from one generation of teachers to the next, most was lost or is now indecipherable. The wisdom that remains you now hold in your hands. Study it carefully, allow it to unfold before you, then apply the principles of HA HA and you will behold the most wondrous gift of all—the Great AHA!

The journey of a thousand smiles begins with a single lighthearted step.

2
Becoming a Laughing Teacher

If you are thinking a year ahead, smile.
If you are thinking ten years ahead, laugh.
If you are thinking one hundred years ahead, teach others to laugh.

By sowing a smile once, you will harvest once.
By planting laughter, you will harvest tenfold.
By teaching others to laugh, you will harvest one hundredfold.
An adaptation of an ancient Chinese poem

What an amazing decision you made when you chose a teaching career. Who could have imagined that it would stretch and challenge you as it has—molding your character, testing your patience, challenging your mind, and offering an unparalleled perspective on the whole spectrum of human behavior. Had you known about the moments of frustration and despair, overwork, underpay, lack of acknowledgment, and administrative red tape, perhaps you would have chosen a different path. But if you had, you would also have turned your back on one of the most rewarding of all human experiences: imparting knowledge to another human being, while serving as a strong role model with the potential of being a lasting influence. How many careers offer such subtle but ongoing reward? Last, but not least, as a teacher you have the power to model an appreciation and joy for life, depending on your approach to that mysterious activity called "teaching."

> **Laughter is by definition healthy.** – Doris Lessing

It has been said that one person's paradise is another's hell, just as one teacher's glory may be another's misery. Although teaching brings with it an unpredictability that makes one year as different as the next, there is one thing that is forever in your hands: your attitude about your students and the learning process.

Education is too important to be taken seriously!

Not long ago, a parent observed two teachers team teaching a seventh-grade social studies class. The classroom was noisy, with frequent disruptions and much commotion. After the hour, one teacher sighed heavily and said to the parent, "These kids are going to drive me to an early grave! Did you notice how often we had to correct them? Thank goodness it's the last period of the day! I think I'm going to need a nap when I get home!" She shuffled out of the room with a forlorn expression and a stooped posture.

Soon after, the second teacher said, "Aren't they great? So high-spirited and full of energy! Right now they're a little scattered, but I plan to teach them how to focus their attention in a meaningful direction. I hope the interruptions weren't too disturbing. It's my goal to get them so involved in the learning process, they won't have time to misbehave!"

When the parent asked the second teacher what her secret was, she said, "My motto is that a laugh each day keeps behavior problems away! It's a big order, which is why I have a whole year to work with them." She walked out of the room with a lightness in her step, whistling and swinging her arms. Within just four minutes, the parent went from despair to feeling elated. There is no doubt about it, enthusiasm and lightheartedness are contagious.

Which teacher would you rather have? More important, how many teachers, from your entire educational experience, can you honestly recall that fit the description of "exceptional, motivating, and enthusiastic, with a sense of humor and playfulness"? The average college graduate has had approximately two hundred teachers, and yet most can't name three teachers who fit the above description. Many can think of only one or two. Some cannot think of a single teacher who fits the description.

This is quite a commentary on how teaching and learning are approached in American schools. Educational pioneer, Italian physician, and child specialist Maria Montessori said, "True learning always takes place in a spirit of joy and abandonment." The good news is that we have an opportunity each year to become memorable, life-changing teachers for our students.

We must ask ourselves as teachers: What is our fundamental attitude toward our

students? Do we believe that they are a delightful group of learners? Or do we see them as an unruly group of troublemakers? Do we see education as a difficult, grueling process, or as an exciting adventure? The level of lightness or gloom in our classroom is a reflection of our attitudes about school and learning. If we perceive that there is never enough time in the day, we communicate panic, frustration, and impatience. If our underlying thought is that teaching is an awful job that is demanding, draining, or even dangerous, we project judgment, rigidity, and fear.

If we believe that education, for the most part, is a stimulating and challenging profession, we project enthusiasm, acceptance, and caring. If we believe that we have enough time to teach our material and make a difference in the lives of our students, we will project an attitude of calm certainty.

One of the fundamental principles in physics states, "Nothing remains stationary. Everything is in the process of growth or decay." With this in mind, we have written this section to help you to determine whether your "fun-damental" attitude in the classroom is a laughing or limiting one. It has been said that enthusiasm and laughter are contagious. The following pages offer some creative ideas to help you to become a laughing teacher who knows how to have sides aching, walls shaking, and brains baking!

Drink deep of living,
Deeper yet of mirth,
For there is nothing
    better than laughter
Anywhere on earth!
    – Frances Frost

**When laughter and education work together,
expect everything!**

3
Pop Quiz

This pop quiz contrasts two different attitudes toward teaching. It is meant to help you determine your dominant attitude toward your work and your students. Sometimes what we think we are projecting is not congruent with how others perceive us. You may believe you are expressing competence and playfulness, while others may feel you are expressing a "cold front with intermittent sarcasm." To communicate effectively and successfully, it's important to know yourself well. One method is to ask for  honest feedback from others; another is to try to see yourself and your attitudes as objectively as you can. Are you a laughing or a limiting teacher? Do students mentally expand or contract when they enter your classroom? Remember that your answers will reflect your mood today. If you take the pop quiz again tomorrow, your results may be different. Take it a few times, and discuss your results with a trusted peer.

Directions: Please read the two phrases that are positioned side by side in the pop quiz. Place a check mark in the box next to the statement that reflects your dominant attitude. Add the check marks to get a subtotal, and continue until you get a grand total. Check your score. (For additional insight, ask one of your teaching colleagues or a special student to rate you on these forty-eight points.)

If you find that over 25 percent of your attitudes fall within the boxes on the right, this strongly indicates that you may be burning out, a condition that can ultimately lead to an early death. Research has recently linked the qualities of anger, irritability, aggression, and overall hostility with coronary arrest. It's not the "hurry" but the "hostility" that kills. This is even more reason to use humor as a method of coping with stress.

Remember, he or she who laughs, lasts!

Pop Quiz:
Laughing Versus Limiting Teaching Style

TRUE   **TRUE**

☐	1. Seeing each learner as an individual	Seeing each learner as a number	1.	☐
☐	2. Sharing knowledge freely and joyously	Imparting information to gain power	2.	☐
☐	3. Teaching with an open heart	Teaching with a closed mind	3.	☐
☐	4. Expecting the best from learners	Expecting the worst from learners	4.	☐
☐	5. Creating the classroom rules together	Dictating the classroom rules	5.	☐
☐	6. Continuing to grow professionally	No longer learning and developing	6.	☐
☐	7. Promoting cooperation in the classroom	Fostering competition in the classroom	7.	☐
☐	8. Helping students learn with ease	Focusing on teaching with ease	8.	☐
☐	9. Believing that your class is the best	Believing that your class is mediocre	9.	☐
☐	10. Teaching with integrity and high ideals	Compromising your teaching ideals	10.	☐
☐	11. Paying attention to the little details about each student	Putting yourself on automatic and overlooking the little details	11.	☐
☐	12. Applauding every small success	Ignoring small successes	12.	☐
☐	13. Facing challenges with courage and humor	Resisting or complaining about challenges	13.	☐
☐	14. Maintaining balance despite the upsets	Making mountains out of molehills	14.	☐
☐	15. Believing it's never too late for any learner	Giving up on unmotivated learners	15.	☐
☐	16. Encouraging classroom spirit and identity	Favoring good learners	16.	☐
☐	17. Expressing yourself within the teacher role	Hiding your identity within your teacher role	17.	☐
☐	18. Enabling learners to see their gifts and talents	Intimidating learners with your talents	18.	☐
☐	19. Believing change is possible	Believing change is impossible	19.	☐
☐	20. Emotionally detaching from things you can't affect	Staying upset about things you can't change	20.	☐
☐	21. Teaching learners to use their power	Teaching learners to rely on your power	21.	☐
☐	22. Working because you love teaching and learning	Working only because you want money and security	22.	☐
☐	23. Keeping learners your top priority	Keeping fact giving as your top priority	23.	☐
☐	24. Exploring new ways to generate enthusiasm	Thinking new teaching methods are a waste of time	24.	☐
☐	25. Modeling high self-esteem and self-respect	Modeling self-criticism and perfectionism	25.	☐
☐	26. Enjoying the uniqueness of each learner	Showing intolerance for differences	26.	☐
☐	27. Creating a positive, visually vibrant learning environment	Being unaware of the quality of your teaching environment	27.	☐
☐	28. Praising learners for their contributions	Expecting rather than praising contributions	28.	☐
☐	29. Trusting your ability to handle difficult situations	Worrying about how to handle difficult situations	29.	☐

☐ **Total Number True**   **Total Number True** ☐

Pop Quiz:
Laughing Versus Limiting Teaching Style

TRUE		**TRUE**
☐ 30. Self-disclosing when appropriate	Feeling awkward about self-disclosure	30. ☐
☐ 31. Measuring success by fulfillment and happiness	Measuring success by results, performance, and struggle	31. ☐
☐ 32. Enjoying the process as well as the goal	Focusing only on the goal	32. ☐
☐ 33. Working toward improving the educational system	Criticizing and complaining about the educational system	33. ☐
☐ 34. Holding an image of learners as successful	Holding an image of learners as limited	34. ☐
☐ 35. Allowing yourself to receive love	Keeping yourself emotionally distant	35. ☐
☐ 36. Focusing on what you want in the classroom	Focusing on what you don't want to happen	36. ☐
☐ 37. Approaching learners in an assertive manner	Aggressively approaching learners	37. ☐
☐ 38. Beginning each day with positive expectancy	Beginning each day with a negative mind-set	38. ☐
☐ 39. Brainstorming in the teachers' lounge	Commiserating in the teachers' lounge	39. ☐
☐ 40. Seeing each class as unique	Comparing classes from year to year	40. ☐
☐ 41. Focusing on the present	Thinking only of retirement	41. ☐
☐ 42. Using humor to help relieve classroom tension	Using sarcasm and ridicule for control	42. ☐
☐ 43. Separating learners from their behavior	Judging and blaming learners for their difficult behavior	43. ☐
☐ 44. Complimenting learners frequently	Looking to find faults in learners	44. ☐
☐ 45. Working for a better tomorrow	Forecasting doom and gloom	45. ☐
☐ 46. Dwelling on what went well at the end of the day	Dwelling on what went wrong at the end of the day	46. ☐
☐ 47. Relaxing and smiling a lot	Looking serious and stressed	47. ☐
☐ 48. Creating a laughing classroom; after all, it's your choice!	Creating a limiting classroom; after all, it's your choice!	48. ☐

[ ] **Total Number True**   **Total Number True** [ ]

Grand Total   **Grand Total**

[ ]   [ ]

Scoring

1–15	It's time to try a few fun new ideas.	**1–15**	It's time to identify and change bad habits.
16–30	Wow! Keep the playful ball rolling.	**16–30**	Whoa! Put the brakes on negativity.
31–40	Congrats! You're on the verge of mastery.	**31–40**	Caution! You're on the verge of burnout.
41–48	You'll soon be voted Teacher of the Year!	**41–48**	Have you thought about humor therapy?

4

Fifty Excuses for Not Laughing

How to Look Like You Were Weaned on a Pickle

1. I tried it once and it didn't work.
2. Our school is highly academic.
3. The students are already hysterical.
4. I will have to ask my principal first.
5. The children might miss their buses.
6. I'm not dressed for the occasion.
7. I don't have time for such nonsense.
8. It's not proper training for the real world.
9. I might get laugh lines.
10. I don't do stand-up comedy.
11. It takes too much preparation.
12. Things are absolutely perfect the way they are.
13. We can't afford to add this to the curriculum.
14. It's not in our school code of ethics.
15. Is this one of those right-brain approaches?
16. I might get calls from irate parents.
17. It could bring on my allergies.
18. We just had the walls painted.
19. I don't have sufficient background.
20. Since I was miserable in school, they'll be miserable.
21. Can't we just buy a laugh track?
22. We're a public school, not a private school.
23. I laugh only in the privacy of my own home.
24. It's way too messy.
25. My students have never seen my teeth.
26. Perhaps after I get my master's degree.
27. I'll bring it to my committee for discussion.
28. Maybe we'll try it as an assignment.
29. If I start laughing, I won't be able to stop.
30. It won't help my students pass their SATs.
31. I'm too old to start laughing now.
32. What do you think school is—a sitcom?
33. What if I lose face?
34. I'd like to read more about it first.
35. Students might assume that life is a big joke.
36. Maybe if I were paid more, I'd reconsider.
37. There's nothing funny about my classroom.
38. My parents never taught me how.
39. It's not statistically sound.
40. I hear that it's bad for the bladder.
41. I'm saving it for summer vacation.
42. I *was* weaned on a pickle!
43. I read that laughter destroys brain cells.
44. Can I get any CEUs for it?
45. The school board will never approve.
46. I don't have enough handouts.
47. You don't understand—I have a bad hip.
48. My laugh sounds like a Canadian goose.
49. My classroom isn't big enough.
50. Gee whiz, it slipped my mind.

Fill in your own: _____

5

Four Humor Styles

What's Your Humor Style?

Humor is a mysterious phenomenon. Ask most teachers if they have a good sense of humor, and 99 percent will respond affirmatively. Moore Colby wrote, "Men will confess to treason, murder, arson, false teeth or a wig, but how many will own up to a lack of humor?" Along the same lines, Steve Allen wrote, "[W]e will accept almost any allegation of our deficiencies—cosmetic, intellectual, virtuous—save one, the charge that we have no sense of humor." To do so could cause great embarrassment, because it might be an admission of a horrible personality flaw, which, if discovered, could result in social ostracism.

If you ask teachers if they know of others who lack a sense of humor, they can probably name a few. Since humor is highly subjective and a matter of personal taste, it's important to remember that what is funny to one person isn't necessarily funny to another. One person may find the slapstick comedy of the Three Stooges outrageously funny, while another enjoys Victor Borge's dry wit. Each generation, each gender, and each culture also differs in what it considers humorous or funny. Although there are differences, humor is universal and exists in some form within all cultures and, hopefully, within the learning environment.

> Humor brings insight and tolerance. Irony brings a deep and less friendly understanding.
> – Agnes Repplier

13

> **Everything is funny as long as it is happening to somebody else.**
> – Will Rogers

There are many "hues" of humor, running across the spectrum from playful, witty, and affectionate to satirical, degrading, and biting. Each type serves a purpose and fulfills a need, whether it's to alleviate pain, discharge nervous excitement, promote bonding, or express anger in a socially acceptable form. Each finds its own outlet or forum, whether through puns, parody, physical comedy, one-liners, shaggy-dog stories, cartoons, or impersonations, to name only a few.

There are two very distinct sides to the humor coin: the comic and the tragic. Humor can act as a social lubricant or a social retardant in the educational setting. It can educate or denigrate, heal or harm, embrace or deface. It's a powerful communication tool, no matter which side is chosen. Ridicule has been used for thousands of years both to maintain the status quo as well as to change it.

To help you identify your humor style, we have devised a system that divides humor styles into four distinct categories–the Joy Master, the Fun Meister, the Joke Maker, and the Life Mocker (see the four-quadrant graphic). As you read through the explanations of each humor style, ask yourself which characteristics best describe your sense of humor. What is your typical reaction when a potentially funny situation occurs in the classroom?

Then think of colleagues you would describe as having little or "no" sense of humor and determine which style(s) they possess. No doubt you will discover that they aren't in the same category as you are. The farther other people are from your style, the more likely you are to experience conflicts with them. Next, ask yourself whether your humor style brings your students closer to you or keeps them at arm's length, whether it enlivens or deadens them, and whether it is helping you to reach your teaching goals. If you are dissatisfied with your answers, it's time to look closely at how to use humor to evoke goodwill rather than provoke hostility. The following quadrant and checklists will give you an insightful start.

> **Humor is our greatest national resource, which must be preserved at all costs.**
> – James Thurber

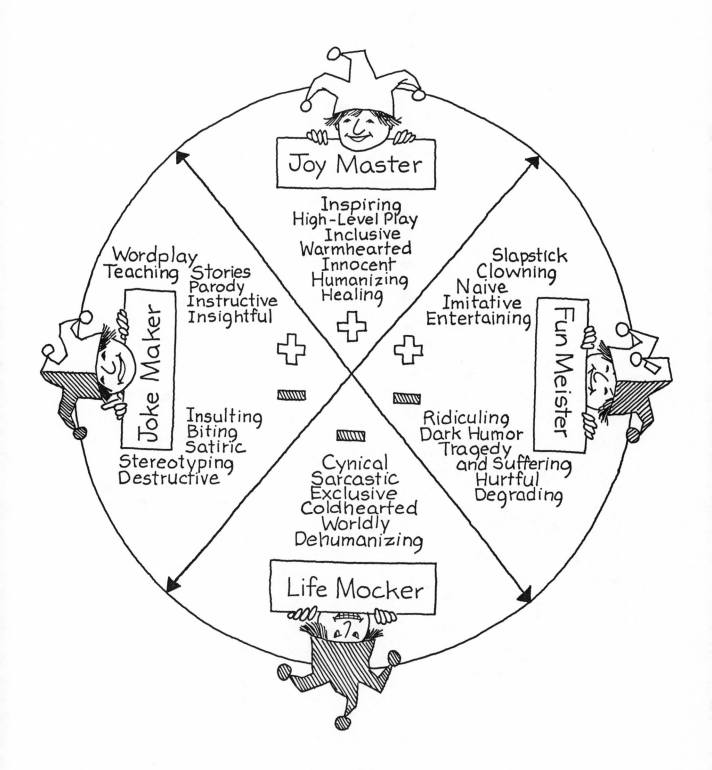

Joy Master

Inspiring
High-Level Play
Inclusive
Warmhearted
Innocent
Humanizing
Healing

Wordplay
Teaching Stories
Parody
Instructive
Insightful

Slapstick
Clowning
Naive
Imitative
Entertaining

Joke Maker

Fun Meister

Insulting
Biting
Satiric
Stereotyping
Destructive

Ridiculing
Dark Humor
Tragedy
and Suffering
Hurtful
Degrading

Cynical
Sarcastic
Exclusive
Coldhearted
Worldly
Dehumanizing

Life Mocker

Joy Master

You can identify Joy Masters by the lightness of their step. Bounding into rooms, they bring with them a sense of positive expectancy. They light up the places they enter, and they usually have a smile for everyone. Joy Masters take humor and play to their highest forms and use them to heal, affirm, uplift, and inspire others.

The joy that Joy Masters impart is infectious. They rise above the doom and gloom projected by others. They laugh for the sheer joy of laughing and have the ability to bring a ray of hope into seemingly hopeless situations. They believe the world is out to do them good and have learned to transform the pain and disappointment of life into positive learning experiences.

When Joy Masters add their traits to the positive traits of a Fun Meister, they engage in high-level play and merriment. They are always good sports and wouldn't consider playing a "practical joke" in case it might inadvertently hurt someone.

When their traits combine with the positive traits of a Joke Maker, they are clever and witty wordsmiths who see humor as a way of teaching and reaching.

Are You a Joy Master?

Use the following checklist to determine your Joy Master skills.

_____1. I bring joy and inspiration to my students.

_____2. My students feel better about themselves after spending time in my classroom.

_____3. I am able to ignite faith, hope, and a sense of optimism in my classroom.

_____4. My playfulness is full of affirmation and acknowledgment of others.

_____5. My sense of humor has a healing effect on those around me.

_____6. Although far from naive, I have a healthy, internalized "second innocence."

_____7. My humor is inclusive and brings those around me closer.

_____8. My sense of humor expands the minds of those around me.

If you have checked five or more of the statements, congratulations! As a Joy Master, you know how to take humor to its highest form! As a role model, your warm sense of humor will be an inspiration to others.

Fun Meister

Fun Meisters are highly entertaining, know how to have a rollicking good time, and want to include you in it. They see the potential for fun in almost every situation, but would never be socially inappropriate just to get a laugh.

Fun Meisters are bold with their humor and laugh loudly and unselfconsciously. They are not afraid to slap their knees or buckle over with laughter. They are usually the life of a party. They never laugh "at" people but "with" them. They giggled a lot as children and find it easy to get down on the floor and play with them. They are everyone's favorite aunt or uncle.

When their positive qualities include the qualities of a Joy Master, Fun Meisters engage in playful, slapstick antics. Many take up clowning as a profession or a hobby.

When Fun Meisters adopt the negative qualities of a Life Mocker, their fun turns against people and becomes degrading and cruel and takes the form of poking fun at and humiliating others.

Are You a Fun Meister?

Use the following checklist to determine your Fun Meister skills.

Positive Traits

_____1. I am considered to be an expressive and funny teacher.

_____2. I use lots of gestures and movement when I am teaching to keep my students' attention.

_____3. I am a natural imitator, and my students often ask me to imitate someone or something.

_____4. I easily and often evoke hearty laughter from my students.

Negative Traits

_____5. My humor style sometimes takes a twist and involves ridiculing others.

_____6. Sometimes my mimicry becomes cruel or humiliating.

_____7. My sense of humor can lean toward the morbid, making light of tragedy and suffering.

_____8. I sometimes regret making humorous and biting comments.

If you have three or more checks in either category, you are definitely a frolicking Fun Meister. Challenge yourself to turn the negative traits into positive ones that can be appreciated by all!

Joke Maker

Joke Makers remember punch lines and know how to weave funny tales that have others wiping away tears of laughter. Their comic timing is impeccable. They have an uncanny ability to use their voice in strange and humorous ways and are good imitators.

Joke Makers like to create funny stories based on their experiences. They pride themselves on being able to see the humor in even their most difficult lessons. You can always rely on a Joke Maker to have a funny turn of phrase, joke, quotation, or story to help you see a situation in a new and different light.

When Joke Makers have the positive qualities of a Joy Master, their jokes are insightful and instructive and can help lift one's spirit. They love to parody things that they find hypocritical.

When Joke Makers combine their characteristics with the qualities of a Life Mocker, their jokes turn ugly, self-deprecating, and bitingly satiric. They use them to vent their rage and hurt others.

Are You a Joke Maker?

Use the following checklist to determine your Joke Maker skills.

Positive Traits

____1. I frequently entertain students with my clever wit.

____2. I often tell jokes to help my students lighten up.

____3. When I tell a good story in my classroom, you can hear a pin drop!

____4. I enjoy clever wordplay with my students.

Negative Traits

____5. My jokes can be off-color or insulting at times.

____6. I am sometimes sarcastic or satirical in my instructional style.

____7. My humor has a tendency to be self-deprecating.

____8. My humor often has a judgmental or critical edge.

If you have three or more checks in either category, you are probably a jovial Joke Maker. Challenge yourself to turn the negative traits into positive ones that will bring a smile to everyone's face.

Life Mocker

Life Mockers take humor to its lowest form and use it to ridicule, shame, and dehumanize others. Life Mockers sneer rather than smile. They consider themselves superior to everyone on the planet. They use their humor as a weapon to destroy feelings of charity and contentment. They live mostly in their intellect and are constantly commenting on what is wrong with the world around them. Life Mockers treat life itself as a joke and dismiss joy and fun as frivolous and childish.

Their idea of a hearty laugh is a "Ha, I told you so" type of laugh. They win the admiration **but not** the affection of their peers through their flippancy and total disregard for life. Like sugarcoated poison, Life Mockers' humor may bring an initial smile, but it ultimately turns people away from them.

When Life Mockers combine their qualities with those of a Fun Meister, they engage in cruel humor disguised as fun. They only laugh deeply when others are hurt or are in pain. They are fond of saying, "What's the matter, can't you take a joke?"

Life Mockers are cynical and sarcastic; when they add their traits to those of a Joke Maker, they use humor to degrade and stereotype and keep people from experiencing their common bonds.

Are You a Life Mocker?

Use the checklist to determine if you are a Life Mocker.

____1. I tend to intimidate students with my sharp tongue and cynicism.

____2. My humor is cold and biting.

____3. I am pessimistic about life and can quickly find fault with any situation.

____4. I am often sarcastic in my day-to-day interactions with students.

____5. I am well respected, but not well liked.

____6. I don't express affection nor do I give compliments in my classroom.

____7. My humor is usually exclusive, intended to divide others through the method of one-upmanship.

____8. I tend to feel superior and have been told that my humor is degrading.

If you have checked five or more of the statements, beware! What you may consider a "sense of humor" is really your method of lashing out at and hurting others. Take time to analyze what messages you are giving to yourself about the world and your place within it. Look at the positive qualities of the Joy Master, Fun Meister, and Joke Maker to see if they can help you become lighter and more loving toward yourself and others.

6

The High Fives of Humor

5
Characteristics of Laughing Teachers

1. Creative use of examples and illustrations.
2. Rich understanding of subject matter.
3. Commitment to lifelong learning.
4. Broad repertoire of teaching techniques.
5. Can motivate and inspire.

5
Positive Results From Laughing

1. Enthusiasm.
2. Confidence.
3. Optimism.
4. Joy.
5. Openness.

5
Qualities That Reflect Fun and Enthusiasm

1. Vocal variety.
2. Animated facial expressions.
3. Exuberant energy level.
4. Passion about the subject being taught.
5. Willingness to take risks.

5
Social Benefits of Laughter

1. Builds a sense of a team.
2. Promotes creativity.
3. Increases communication.
4. Enhances self-esteem.
5. Reduces conflict.

5
Fun Things Teachers Enjoy About Teaching

1. Empowering others.
2. Autonomy.
3. Children.
4. Learning.
5. Summer vacation.

5
Funny Little Requirements Needed to Become a Teacher

1. A teaching certificate.
2. A love for children.
3. Fortitude.
4. Organizational skills.
5. A strong immune system.

5
Physical Benefits of Laughter

1. Reduces stress.
2. Enhances immune system functioning.
3. Acts as an internal massage.
4. Regulates blood pressure.
5. Feels good.

5
Fun Things Teachers Do With Their Spare Time

1. What spare time?

5
Ways to Recognize Laughter

1. Exhalation of breath.
2. Shaking of chest and sides.
3. Watering eyes.
4. Contraction of facial muscles.
5. Cheeks turning bright red

5
Basic Competencies Enhanced by Humor

1. Communication skills.
2. Creative/critical thinking skills.
3. Cultural awareness skills.
4. Cooperative learning skills.
5. Coping skills.

5
Things We Should Say to Laughing Teachers

1. Thank you!
2. Just how do you do it?
3. You're a fantastic educator and great humanitarian.
4. You deserve a raise.
5. Keep up the great work!

7

The Laughing Classroom Oath

To be stated while wearing a great big grin:

I, _____ ,

Do solemnly swear from this day forward
To grease my giggling gears each day
And to wear a grin on my face for no reason at all!
I promise to tap my funny bone often,
With my students and colleagues,
And to laugh at least fifteen times per day.
I believe that frequent belly laughter
Cures terminal tightness, cerebral stiffness,
And hardening of the attitudes,
And that HA HA often leads to AHA!
Therefore, I vow, from this day forth,
To brighten the day of everyone I meet,
And to laugh long and prosper!

8

Song: "The Laughter Rap"

This information is intended to be read aloud rap style, while listeners snap their fingers to the beat and make rap sounds if they choose!

Your brain's a be-bopping,
Never-stopping machine,
A neural circuit, circus –
You call your "noggin" your "bean."
It turns on and off at a megarate,
As chemical impulses reverberate,
And flow, to show
The pituitary gland has been stimulated.
Now there's a gland that's been underrated –
How else would survival be communicated?
Hormones and endorphins
Race through your blood –
Over hill, over dale, keep your eye on the flood.
Your pulse rate and blood pressure
Climb the tall ladder.
You're feeling really fine, but keep track of your bladder.
Your temperature rises half a degree.
Your internal landlord turns up the heat for free.
Your vocal chords quiver, and your face contorts,
And the pout you've been sprouting that says you're out of sorts
Takes a hike, takes a trip,
Leaves town.
And the smile you've been hiding
Moves in and wins – hands down.
Your arteries and muscles expand and contract,
Then pressure builds in your air culs-de-sac.
From your mouth, your lips, your teeth and tongue,
At seventy miles per hour, a laughter shower gets flung.
Don't glower – there's power in a laugh.
It's an inner upper –
It's more filling than a seven-course supper.
So stretch those fourteen muscles and smile.
If you do, I'm with you,
'Cause you've got style!

9
Humor Homework

1. Identify your humor style and the humor styles of your faculty.

2. Make copies of the Laughing Classroom Oath and distribute them to your faculty. Find one or two others to take the oath with you.

3. Have your class perform "The Laughter Rap." Write new verses for it.

4. Ask a colleague if he or she would be willing to become your laughing buddy. Form larger coalitions and give yourselves titles such as "The Three Wise Guys."

5. Talk with your class about the various styles of humor. Create a written agreement with them that they will not use humor to hurt one another. Have them sign it and post it in a visible area.

10
Play Sheet

1. Name your three favorite teachers.
   How is your teaching style similar
   to that of these three role models?

2. What qualities set them apart from the others?

3. From the perspective of a learner, how did these teachers make you feel about
   yourself and about learning?

4. Which of their techniques or attitudes would you like to adapt and incorporate
   into your teaching style?

5. What style of humor do you appreciate the most? List several things you feel are
   funny and not funny and analyze why this is so.

11
Notes for Myself

Creating
a
Laughing Classroom

Part Two

12

Paula Parrot and the Carrot

"So, tell me, Paula," said her teacher, "what would you like to learn?"

The question startled Paula. Her eyes grew wide. She cocked her head to the left side and stared at her teacher. A thirty-degree tilt of her head usually gave Paula the perspective she needed to answer intelligently. She cocked her head to the right side when she noticed that her left side wasn't working. She kept cocking her head, hoping to shake the answer loose.

The question posed to Paula was more difficult for her to answer than "What do you want to be when you grow up?" Adults always asked this inane question at the most awkward moments. "Alive! Alive!" she'd reply. She knew an answer was right if no one could argue with it. Paula thought that asking what she wanted to learn was a trick question similar to "What do you do for a living?" She knew that it would take her many years to find the answer to that convoluted question.

After much thought, Paula decided that the question was a conundrum given to her to teach her to move beyond thinking. It didn't make sense because she hadn't learned to think properly yet, so Paula tucked her head inside her wing and drifted off to sleep.

Her teacher sang the question softly so as not to disturb Paula's reverie. "Paula, what would you like to learn?"

Her teacher's persistence was too much for Paula to bear. She would have to find an inarguable answer to be left at peace. Paula ruffled her feathers, preened, turned several times on her perch, and then sat very still. Finally, Paula squawked what she believed was the perfect retort—a retort based upon years of experience: "What you want me to learn—what you want me to learn." She waited for her teacher to bob her head up and down in a display of approval.

Her teacher quickly responded, "I want you to learn what you want to learn."

The ball was back in Paula's court. Paula was expecting an ordinary aviary and wasn't prepared for her teacher's new twist. Paula curled her claw and tucked it up in her feathers. She hoped that standing on one leg would help her gain insight into her teacher's intolerable question. It was intolerable because it appeared unanswerable.

Paula remembered that when she was very young, she learned how to sit still, silent, and stiff. Her next teacher insisted that she stretch her wings and participate. Paula obliged and became animated. The next year, her new teacher wanted her to learn how to behave, and the year after that, she learned lessons in cooperation. By the fifth year, Paula had discovered how to determine what her teacher wanted her to learn. This was easy, she thought, for it took so little thinking. But this time, she could not comprehend her teacher's true motive.

The question disturbed Paula deeply. She paced back and forth, picked and pulled at her feathers, and thought so long and hard that she began to molt. With feathers flying everywhere, all she could say was, "I don't know! I don't know!"

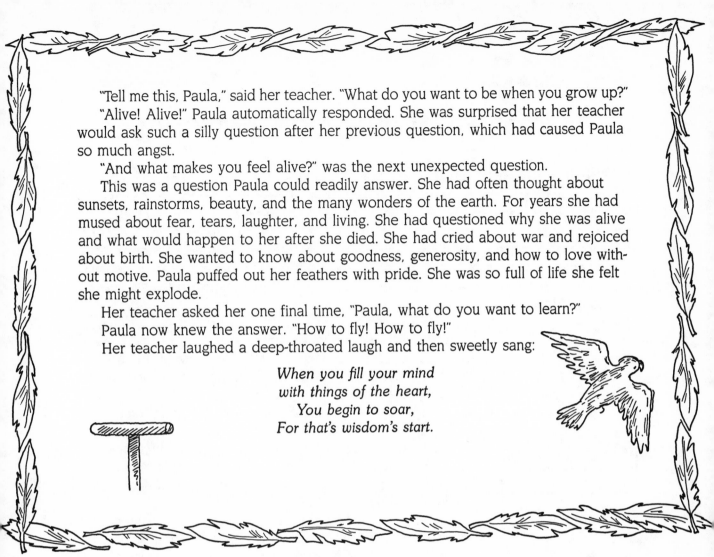

"Tell me this, Paula," said her teacher. "What do you want to be when you grow up?"

"Alive! Alive!" Paula automatically responded. She was surprised that her teacher would ask such a silly question after her previous question, which had caused Paula so much angst.

"And what makes you feel alive?" was the next unexpected question.

This was a question Paula could readily answer. She had often thought about sunsets, rainstorms, beauty, and the many wonders of the earth. For years she had mused about fear, tears, laughter, and living. She had questioned why she was alive and what would happen to her after she died. She had cried about war and rejoiced about birth. She wanted to know about goodness, generosity, and how to love without motive. Paula puffed out her feathers with pride. She was so full of life she felt she might explode.

Her teacher asked her one final time, "Paula, what do you want to learn?"

Paula now knew the answer. "How to fly! How to fly!"

Her teacher laughed a deep-throated laugh and then sweetly sang:

> *When you fill your mind*
> *with things of the heart,*
> *You begin to soar,*
> *For that's wisdom's start.*

A grimace or a grin – how will your day begin?

31

13

Creating a Laughing Classroom

Creating a laughing classroom offers one guarantee: positive unpredictability. When learners gather together in the spirit of play, the walls expand, the ceiling lifts, differences begin to dissolve, and a tremendous sense of "mental mobility" abounds. Risks become adventures, and even the most timid students may answer questions or surprise everyone by revealing hidden talents. Outrageous streaks of genius emerge without self-consciousness, and both the teacher and learner become receptive to exploring new possibilities. The process of learning is no longer perceived as "dread-ucation."

Unextinguished laughter
shakes the skies.
– Homer

Diane had the chance to experience what a difference laughter can make. She was required to take eight hours of "traffic school" to clean her slate of a minor traffic offense. Several friends warned her to prepare for the longest, most boring learning experience of her life. Two weeks before the class began, she heard that a local comedy group was licensed to teach the course she was scheduled to take, with one vital difference—they designed it with the reluctant learner in mind. They planned to incorporate humor, acting, jokes, and music into the day.

As promised, the day was full of laughter and group participation. By midmorning, Diane had scored 100 percent on the morning quiz and had laughed so hard that her face ached. To overcome the midafternoon slump, the instructor dressed up as a traffic officer and acted out traffic scenarios. He had the class create and present a mock traffic debate, which had them rolling in the aisles. It was a thrill for her to see how masterfully humor could be mixed with sizable amounts of information. She left the class refreshed and inspired—with forty new friends. She easily recalls the information she learned and is glad to have seen the speed with which laughter promoted learning.

Laughter is a great gift that we can give to our students and an important skill that we can model. When learners develop the ability to take themselves lightly, learning becomes a joyous experience, not a dreaded one. There are many educational, physical, and psychological benefits of laughter and play.

Without love and laughter there is no joy; live amid love and laughter.
– Horace

Here are a few of the major benefits you and your students will gain if you include laughter and play as an integral part of your day. Laughter and play will:

- maintain a high attention level,
- relieve physical and mental stress,
- build rapport,
- increase retention,
- enhance self-esteem,
- promote divergent thinking,
- bring new insights,
- allow for pleasurable learning, and
- increase a feeling of hope.

This chapter is full of hands-on ways to incorporate humor into your learning environment. Don't wait for laughter in the hereafter; use laughter in the here and now.

Laughter says, "Come take my hand, and together we'll expand."

14

The Laughing Classroom Quiz

Directions: It has been said that the proof is in the pudding. If you need proof beyond the attitudes of your students and the atmosphere in your classroom to gauge the level of playfulness, take this Laughing Classroom Quiz.

YES NO

☐ ☐ 1. My students are enthusiastic as they enter my room.

☐ ☐ 2. My students have a few affectionate nicknames for me.

☐ ☐ 3. My students feel free to ask questions during class.

☐ ☐ 4. My students laugh often and appropriately in the classroom.

☐ ☐ 5. My students smile and say hello to me in the halls.

☐ ☐ 6. My students work well together when working in small groups.

☐ ☐ 7. My students are disappointed if a substitute fills in for me.

☐ ☐ 8. Occasionally a former student will come back to visit with me.

☐ ☐ 9. Students often recommend me to their peers.

☐ ☐ 10. My students are willing to share personal information when appropriate.

☐ ☐ 11. My students enjoy sharing small talk with me before or after class.

☐ ☐ 12. My students feel comfortable coming to me for advice.

☐ ☐ 13. My students seem curious about me and my life.

☐ ☐ 14. My classroom atmosphere is interesting and alive.

☐ ☐ 15. I often go beyond the call of duty in my classroom.

☐ ☐ 16. My classroom is a balance between playfulness and discipline.

☐ ☐ 17. I use spontaneous classroom moments whenever time permits.

☐ ☐ 18. I often compliment my students and my entire class.

☐ ☐ 19. I take genuine delight in all my students.

☐ ☐ 20. My students take genuine delight in me.

☐ ☐ 21. There is a sense of family in my classroom.

Scoring

Give yourself one point for each yes answer.

Hot: 18–21

Your classroom has a happy camper attitude. Although you're not without challenges, you certainly encourage the love of learning. The atmosphere in your classroom is warm and safe, and all who enter through your door feel as though they are a part of a family. For some of your students, your classroom is the only healthy family they've known. Congratulations! You are making a difference.

Warm: 13–17

Your classroom is definitely above average in mood and rapport. In fact, for many of your students, it may be their favorite class. Keep up the good work and enthusiastic attitude.

Lukewarm: 7–12

Your classroom has its moments–some memorable and some awful, but mostly just ordinary moments, one after another. Do something unexpected. Surprise yourself, and watch the energy level rise before your very eyes.

Cold: 0–6

Your classroom needs a transfusion. Students are no doubt disenchanted, dull, and disinterested. Ask yourself if you still have any interest in the subject you are teaching. Share more of yourself with your students, and begin to put more of yourself into your work. Small efforts will pay off with big dividends and large grins soon.

A laugh a day keeps the "blah" humbugs away!

15

Fast and Fun: Thirty Ideas

The following fix-it-with-humor remedies will help you to grease the giggling gears when the going gets tough. Some of them we have tried with success. Teachers we have worked with have contributed the other ideas. Adapt, adopt, improvise, or steal these ideas outright! Your grinning students will be glad you did!

1. A Nose for Seriousness

When things start to get too serious during science class, I quietly put on my trusty banana nose. This is a cue for students to start thinking up unusual questions that relate to the subject matter under discussion. If they don't drum up any right away, I start asking bizarre questions to stir their imaginations. Believe it or not, this has dramatically improved retention and triggered a lot of laughter! My students refer fondly to this unusual behavior as "Going Bananas With Questions!"

2. An Upbeat Entrance

Each day, as students file into class, I play three minutes of wonderful upbeat music, such as the theme from *Chariots of Fire* or *Rocky*. I collect various styles of music, so that students never know which one will be playing as they enter my vibrant, alive atmosphere. As my students have become accustomed to this creative new habit, I have found that they mime the lyrics and gesture dramatically to the beat. This lightens up the whole room between classes and sets an invigorating tone.

3. Sherlock's Search

Every Friday afternoon shortly before the bell rang, my third graders and I performed our dreaded weekly ritual—desk check! I'd examine all the desks to see if they were neat and orderly for the following week. It was a tense and unpleasant time for all. One weekend, while watching a Sherlock Holmes movie, I had an idea. The following week, I livened up our desk check by dressing up as Sherlock! I inspected each desk with my magnifying glass, checking carefully as my students

laughed and made comments, such as, "Mr. Holmes, don't forget to look over here!" Needless to say, it has become an anticipated event. Some of my previously untidy students are already cleaning up Thursday afternoon. Others leave Sherlock small notes and treats in their desks. Perhaps this is their way of rewarding me for turning toil into togetherness!

4. Rap It to Me!

Monday morning announcements have always been on my "necessary evils" list, along with cockroaches, household dust, and alarm clocks! Most of my students were becoming masters at distracting themselves, rolling their eyes back into their heads, or listening with one ear while I announced the dreary demands, shoulds, musts, and don'ts. Because I teach in a school where rap music is popular, I decided to go from "bad to rad" Monday mornings. I now give the classroom announcements wearing a flashy metallic purple wig, which the kids especially enjoy because Mother Nature was on strike when it came to hair distribution and my head! I give all the announcements *rap*

style, complete with my students making various sound effects. Vive la différence! They easily remember what was said. Some of them go on singing it under their breaths for the rest of the week. What more could a middle-aged, tone-deaf teacher ask for!

5. Say It Again, Ma'am!

I am a firm believer in positive communication, which is why I have become a voluntary guinea pig in my senior high classroom. Anytime my students catch me saying something in a negative way, such as, "We must hurry, or we'll never finish," they have permission to stop me by saying, "Reframing time-out!" Whenever this happens, I hold an empty frame around my face, and I repeat my message in a positive way, such as, "Let's all concentrate so that we finish on time!" This is always accompanied by smiles and laughter, but even more important, it teaches the valuable skill of reframing and builds rapport between teacher and student.

6. Give It Back to Me!

This review game has been a great way to provide my ninth graders with some movement, laughter, and bonding with one another, while they review important material for upcoming tests. I have students pair off, with student number one facing student number two's back. When I ask a review question, student number one must silently spell out the answer in large exaggerated motions on student number two's back, using just one finger. Student number two then writes down the answer he or she "felt." After asking ten questions, the teams review the answers together, which always generates a lot of interest and laughter. I proceed to give the correct answers, and the review teams can then check my answers against their own. If there is time, I have the teams reverse roles and we go through ten more questions.

7. Blossoming Brains

Horticulture has always been a strong interest of mine. Recently, due to a happy accident, I thought of a way to include it in my tenth-grade math classes. After the holidays, my spouse was about to throw away a poinsettia that appeared to be dying. I insisted that with proper care it could be revived. "Then revive it somewhere else!" was all the enthusiasm she could muster. So revive it, I did! Right in my math classroom! The plant generated so much interest that I soon had a whole table full of plants that thrived in my classroom. Many of my students brought in plant food and various accessories to help the plants along, as well as cuttings from home and an occasional new plant. I was soon bringing in a bouquet of flowers each week. The joy and beauty these plants added to the room each day made up for their minimal cost and care many times over!

8. Crayon Craze

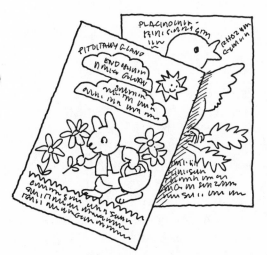

Take simple line drawings from children's coloring books, and type or print any information that you want students to remember in the picture. Photocopy them, pass them out, and use them as review sheets. Pass out crayons, and let students color in the sheets as they review. Research shows that color and simple shapes trigger photographic memory. This simple and fun activity will assist students in remembering material and bring back very fond memories. I have had a positive response from all ages, including adult groups, when I've used this activity for review.

9. Positive Graffiti Board

My high school students love bulletin boards. Unfortunately, they have a habit of focusing on the negative more than the positive, so I created a bulletin board filled only with positive news clippings, great slogans, and memorable events. I was amazed how well it worked. It has become a permanent corner in my room, and students often wander over to read the latest good news. Each week, I include a large blank sheet of paper so students can add phrases, slogans, or ideas to it. This has inspired my class and has given me a needed lift.

10. Silent Laughing Buddy

Write the names of your students on small pieces of paper, and place them in a bowl. Pass the bowl, and have each student pick one name, other than his or her own name, from the bowl. These students then become the "silent laughing buddies" of those whose names they've chosen. It's the responsibility of the silent buddies to keep their chosen buddies laughing by using notes, jokes, and other little surprises for the designated length of time
(one month is recommended). Each person in class has an opportunity to give and receive, simultaneously. It's a great bonding activity, because most students can keep their identity a secret. As the month progresses, the silent laughing buddies may start to give their partners clues to their identity. On the last day, students reveal their identities to their buddies. *Note:* You may want to set ground rules about appropriate and inappropriate surprises.

11. Klutz to the Rescue!

One night, while out with some friends, I learned a simple coin trick. The next day, I showed my students the trick without showing them how it was done. For days, they begged me to reveal my amateur secrets. I finally gave in. This generated so much enthusiasm that I decided to learn one new trick per week. Although, as a budding beginner, I've had my awkward moments performing the coin tricks, my students look forward to these weekly sessions with great interest. At the end of each month, they vote on which trick they liked the most. I give them the answer to only one trick per month because magicians must not reveal all their secrets. I have purchased several do-it-yourself books and now have enough material to last for the year!

12. Special Dress Day

I adapted this idea after I walked into my local bank and discovered everyone was wearing pajamas. When I asked what the occasion was, I was told it was "sleepers' day." I decided to adapt this idea for use in my classroom! On the third Friday of every month, we choose a dress theme and come to school dressed as the part. We call it, "Come as You Aren't Day." We've had Silly Hats Day, Favorite Color Day, Western Day, Patriot Day, Strange Socks Day, and we're still coming up with new

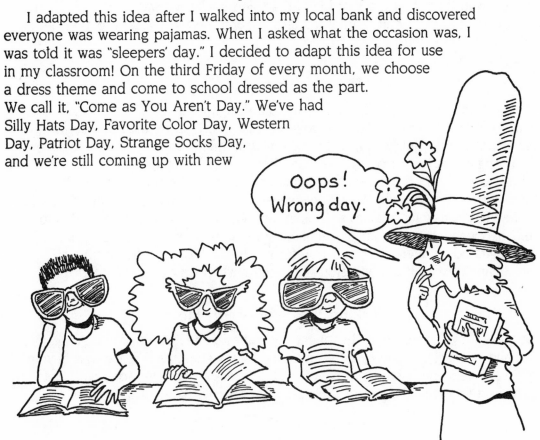

themes for the future. Although not all students participate each time, half of the fun is seeing who will come to school dressed in costume. Sometimes, it has been the least expected students. I have seen students become more creative, less inhibited, and make new friends through the whimsy that this activity triggers!

13. Black "Bored" Blues

I teach seventh-grade math at a large middle school. The most difficult part of teaching math is convincing the students that they have the brainpower to comprehend the lessons and motivating them to actually enjoy the process. So, every morning before I start the lesson, I write in very large letters on the blackboard: "MATH IS FUN!" This has become an opening ritual that my classes enjoy. One day, I was about five minutes late for my first class. When I entered my room, someone had printed "MATH IS FUN" on the blackboard. All I needed to do was add the exclamation point. The ritual took on a life of its own when someone added the letter "E" onto

41

the end of the word FUN, which changed the word to FUN-E! At the end of the class, I showed them that the word FUN-E spelled backward was E-NUF. So, at the end of every lesson, students know the lesson is finished if I write in big letters on the blackboard the word E-NUF!

14. Relaxing in Style

A few years ago, I successfully led my junior high math classes through short, five-minute relaxation exercises. I discovered that many of my students performed better, especially on quizzes, after taking a few moments to relax beforehand. One day, I brought in a lamp from home, complete with colored light bulbs. My students loved it! Now we dim the fluorescent lights and relax to the hue of green, blue, or another pastel-colored bulb. We do this several times a week, and students ask for it if a few days pass and we haven't taken any time to relax. After doing this for a while, I happened to read that pastel shades are sometimes painted on prison walls to calm agitated inmates. Although I prefer not to think of my classroom as a prison, I can attest to the mood shift that occurs when I turn on my lamp.

15. Taking the School Pet Home

Because I love stuffed toys, I brought my stuffed penguins, Frick and Frack, into my second-grade class. They were such a hit with my students that we now have a ritual. Every weekend, a student takes Frick and Frack home. On Monday, the student gives a short report to the rest of the class about the weekend. This activity is

wonderful because it gives students a chance to talk in front of their peers, experience the excitement and privilege of taking care of the classroom pets (a job they take very seriously), and exercise their imaginations while entertaining the rest of us. Recently, one of my students told the class, "Frick and Frack had a great weekend until we went to Grandma's. They ate too much of Grandma's food, and Frack threw up in the car on the way home!" Their stories would present stiff competition for any stand-up comic.

16. Compliments Unlimited

Because I believe in the power of catching my students doing something good, I cut thirty-five shapes from colored paper each week: red apples, yellow corn cobs, green shamrocks, and so forth. All of my thirty-five students receive a colorful cutout

sometime during the week, along with a short note complimenting them on something positive that they did. I place the notes in their desks, on their lunch boxes, in their coat pockets, or in other personal spots where they'll find them. They **are** delighted to find these little notes and anticipate finding them throughout the week.

A few months ago, they initiated cutouts for me. Now, I occasionally find little complimentary notes from students in my coat pocket, taped next to the light switch, and, recently, under my car's windshield wiper. What a delightful way this has been for us to appreciate the little things that too often go unnoticed!

17. Funny Pens and Other Unusual Objects

I have a reputation with my high school students for having the strangest pens and toys in town! From bizarre-looking eraser heads, fluorescent-colored wild animal pens, and intriguing windup toys, you'd think I was managing a toy shop instead of teaching a biology class. My students, however, encourage and reinforce my childlike hobby. At the beginning of each day, they wander over to my desk to see if I have

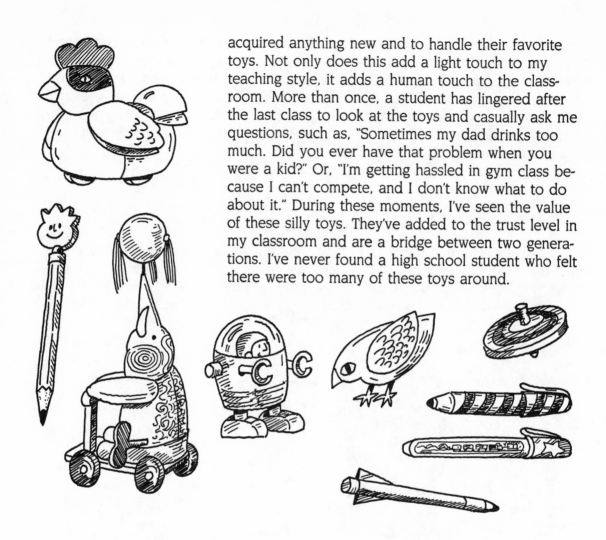

acquired anything new and to handle their favorite toys. Not only does this add a light touch to my teaching style, it adds a human touch to the classroom. More than once, a student has lingered after the last class to look at the toys and casually ask me questions, such as, "Sometimes my dad drinks too much. Did you ever have that problem when you were a kid?" Or, "I'm getting hassled in gym class because I can't compete, and I don't know what to do about it." During these moments, I've seen the value of these silly toys. They've added to the trust level in my classroom and are a bridge between two generations. I've never found a high school student who felt there were too many of these toys around.

18. Here Comes the Sub!

I am a substitute art teacher. Anyone who has worked as a sub knows how difficult it can be to keep control of a class that is determined to take advantage of your vulnerable position. I have created a simple way to stop the creative sabotage from getting a foothold. I stand at the door and greet the students as they enter. I make eye contact with each student and intuitively pick the five or so students (leaders) that I sense might be the first to create the free-for-all atmosphere that I'm trying to prevent. I can usually spot them by their mischievous grins or their "don't mess with me" nonverbal posturing. I start everyone working on a project, and then I immediately go to those potentially "problematic" students and offer them personal help with their work. I spend a few minutes with each student whom I've identified. I haven't had a discipline problem since I started "lending a helping hand" to those students who crave attention.

19. Classroom Trivia

My high school class relishes this half-hour game that we play once a month. I keep some three-by-five-inch cards in a box on my desk. Whenever students get the urge, they write a classroom trivia question on the front of the card, with the answer on the back. The questions may cover a wide range of topics, from tidbits of information about students to classroom trivia. There is only one rule: Trivia submitted must be funny, interesting, or unusual, not personal, negative, or gossip related.

Examples

Q: Who has the oldest living great-grandmother?
A: Allison. Her great-grandmother was ninety-seven last week.
Q: Who takes the longest bus ride here each day?
A: Carlos. He lives almost sixty miles away from school.

This activity is as informative as it is entertaining. Try it yourself!

20. A Wide Range of Rearranging

Every few weeks, I make it a habit to rearrange something in my classroom. Sometimes it's something as simple as a wastebasket, a plant, or the side of the board that I use for announcements. Other times, it's something more noticeable, such as pictures on the wall, the clock, the bulletin board, my desk, or the students'

desks. I tell my students there is an element of delight in the unpredictable, which is part of what life is about. Once in a while, I rearrange something a bit more daring, such as my outfit for the day (i.e., putting it on backward), my hairstyle, my tone of voice, my accent, or my style of teaching! For those students who have a difficult time adjusting to the changes, I simply tell them that this is a golden opportunity to develop a vital skill: the ability to adapt playfully.

21. A Step in the Right Direction

I firmly believe in the power of play as a tool for learning. As a third-grade teacher, I'm grateful that my students still can play and act "silly." One of their favorite ways to review informa-tion is a game that combines "Red Light, Green Light" and "Hangman." I create a series of fifty or more review ques-tions that we must answer as a class. The class deter-mines the place in the room where I will begin and the place where I will finish. Sometimes I start at the back of the room and finish in the hall,

Ben, what's seven times eight?

which always gets a laugh. To begin the game, I ask the predetermined questions, and for every correct answer, I move one step forward. For each incorrect answer, I move one step backward. I become a "human chess piece" at the playful mercy of my students. For variety, I choose a student to move forward or backward during our review session.

22. What's Morton Up To?

In my education classes, I sometimes bring out a life-sized puppet monkey named Morton. Morton's arms wrap around my neck and stick together with velcro, and I use one of my arms to move Morton's mouth. Morton represents the "monkey who hangs on our backs" and gives us negative messages about why we're not  good enough, why our ideas will never work, or why the blame belongs to someone else. Morton and I converse, but I interpret what Morton says because he speaks silently. Messages of encouragement for my students underlie the dialogue, but it is flavored with such a strong dose of candid humor that the students wholeheartedly accept them. In fact, if Morton hasn't made an appearance for a while, my students ask where he's been hanging out.

23. Student Show Time

What hidden talents abound in your classroom? Amaze and inspire one another by having an hour of Student Show Time, once a month. Have students sign up for five to ten minute time slots to share any talents they choose. I have been delighted by the vast array of talent that I've seen during our hour shows. Here are some examples:

47

poetry reading, short story reading, music recitals, singing, dancing, comedy, photography, crafts, theater, song writing, sharing hobbies or collections, or sharing real life stories and adventures (these can include trips). For a hilarious twist, you can include "untalent or almost talent" slots, too, which can include off-key singing, bad acting, bad photography, bad comedy, and any other "untalent" that students may wish to spoof!

24. "Prop-Pourri"

More than once, I have been accused of having a zany personality. Maybe it's because of the many unusual props (including hats, masks, noses, clever pointers, scarves, and capes) that I keep in my classroom. Because the collection was getting out of hand, I brought in an old wooden chest that I keep on the floor near my desk. When the lesson calls for a prop or when I want to make a special point, I creak open the "prop-pourri" chest and look for the right item. My students begin laughing before they know what I'll choose. Sometimes, for special activities and announcements, I allow students to use items from my collection.

25. Nonsense Sayings

Don't let anyone fool you into thinking that taking tests is anything but stressful. I allow my high school English classes five minutes of play before any test to relieve the stress that always accompanies test taking. This idea has worked so well as a tension reducer that I now start every class with five minutes of playtime. I have a special ritualistic saying that cues them that they are going to have a test. I say, "Only because I love you more than life itself: Take out a piece of paper and a writing utensil." Once a student responded, "I wish you wouldn't love us so much!" I often interject other fun, nonsensical sayings into my teaching day. If we are covering difficult or boring material, I start with, "Son of a gun, we're going to have fun, on the bayou." When students don't respond, I say, "I don't know. I give up. What do I win? I'll take the washer, I'll take the dryer, I'll spin again, Vanna" (high school students love contemporary references). To end a class I say, "Do you have any questions? (Pause.) Do you have any answers? Do you want to sing? Do you want to dance? Do you want to cha, cha cha?" No matter how often my students hear these sayings, they always laugh! Some students have even created nonsense sayings of their own.

26. Wake-up Call

All teachers know there's a wide range of energy levels in their classrooms that are dependent upon the time of day. To compensate for these variations, I take a "sleepiness/ wakefulness" survey before I begin teaching a new class for the quarter. I ask students to raise their hands if they consider themselves A.M. or P.M. people. (A.M. people leap out of bed at 5:30 A.M., they pour milk into their cereal bowls and not on the floor, they can hold an intelligent conversation about quantum physics before 8:00 A.M., and so on. P.M. people show signs of life after noon, they start to function about 7:00 P.M., and they do their best work about midnight.) Then I write an A.M. or a P.M. next to their names in my class book. Because the P.M. people usually nod off during class in the morning (no matter how much they pretend to be awake) and the A.M. people have a lull in the afternoon, I have a fun reminder to keep everyone awake. I have a telephone in my desk and underneath it is a very loud battery-operated ringer. When I sense that a student is losing consciousness, I take out the phone and press the buzzer. Then I hand the phone to the sleepy student and say, "It's for you. It's your wake-up call!" Because this is done in the spirit of play and not as a form of ridicule, my students love it. They also know that I can very accurately assess when they are "zoning out." They have tended to be much more alert since I started the wake-up call game.

27. Dream-a-Theme

I believe that imagining and dreaming are essential aspects of learning that are sadly lacking in our educational approach today. So, each week in my classroom, we dream a theme that relates to the world, such as, "Imagine a world with plenty of food for all," "Imagine a world where everybody tells the truth," or "Imagine a world that raises all children with great love and care." We write our dream theme for the week on the board, and, when relevant, we relate all discussions and subject matter to the theme. This has added an element of richness and global perspective to the lessons in ways that have exceeded my expectations. The idea for this activity was inspired by a comment by D. H. Lawrence: "If you don't have a dream, how can you have a dream come true?"

28. Teacher Interview

As a substitute high school teacher, walking into a new classroom on the first day can be a less-than-friendly experience; in fact, it can be downright hostile! This is why I developed a technique that guarantees immediate, high-level interest and rapport. With my initial introduction and announcements, I make the following agreement with my students. If they will agree to answer my questions and help me to feel at home in their classroom, I will, in turn, answer all their questions and help them to feel at home with me. Then I give the students about five minutes to ask me any questions about myself they would like, as long as they are not too personal. Here are a few of the most frequently asked questions: Are you married? Do you have kids? Do you get along with your kids? How old were you when you first fell in love? Did you ever fail a class or a grade? Did you ever drink or take drugs? What are you most proud of that you have done? These questions are foremost in their minds. And the result? A memorable day or week with high rapport! After the interview, I become a real person to them and not an impersonal sub.

29. The Question Is the Answer!

I am a high school science teacher with nearly a world record for the greatest number of strange pop quizzes given to students during a semester. Because I was tired of multiple-choice exams, I created several challenging tests that my students don't loathe taking. The most popular tests are take-offs on television game shows. The most popular pop quiz parody is based on the game show "Jeopardy." I make a list of answers, and I have the students write the questions to those answers. I've used this method for written and oral exams, and with a randomly chosen "panel." The whole class gets a grade based upon the panel's ability to create the right question for the answer I've given.

30. Say Cheese, Please!

Have you ever noticed how people brighten up when they see photos of themselves? After attending a Polaroid workshop for teachers last year, I took pictures of my unsuspecting students a few times a week and placed them on my "Come See the Family Shots" board. I snap about twenty-four photos per month, so the cost is minimal, but the return is maximal. Students from other classes often hover in the corner to see the latest pictures of their classmates. The board brings a playful family atmosphere to my classroom and generates lots of enthusiasm! At the end of each month, I give students their pictures. For many, it is the only photo that has been taken of them in some time. Last year, one of my ninth-grade boys was struck and killed by a car. I presented a beautiful photo of him, grinning from ear to ear, to the bereaved family. His mother dried her eyes and said, "Oh, that's the smile I most wanted to remember! We'd never captured it on film. How can I ever thank you?" This is just one of many rewards I've received from a whim I chose to act upon last year.

16

Twenty-five Ways to Go the Extra Smile

Come disguised as a fire hydrant. 	Glue yourself to the blackboard. 	Make eraser earmuffs and wear them when your class gets noisy. 
Make a three-dimensional bulletin board, complete with laser light show. 	Bring your favorite stuffed animal to class. 	Teach standing at a 30 degree angle. 
Arrange the desks vertically. 	Have students wear prism glasses for a day. 	Fill the garbage can with hot water and soak your feet. 
Bring in a special effects machine to simulate a typhoon. 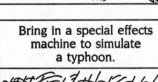	Dress as a referee and throw penalty flags for bad behavior. 	Make forts by covering the desks with blankets. 

Do the end-of-the day chores at the beginning of the day.

Ask students to buckle up instead of buckle down.

Have recess all day, and take a fifteen-minute break for class.

Do we have to play some more?

Have students come dressed as their favorite tree.

Make enough popcorn to fill the entire room.

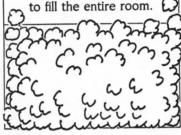

Have students give reports standing in front of a microphone.

And, now, something from the Mesozoic era.

Bring pillows to class, and teach lying down.

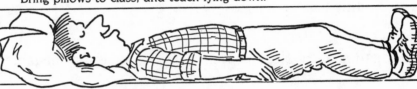

Now, watch me carefully, class, and take notes.

Give the answers to a test, and let the students make up the questions.

And the last answer is "Lunch."

Have students bring all their pets to class on the same day.

Teach while trying to escape from a straitjacket.

Dig a hole in the floor.

Conduct your class as if it were an opera.

stalagmites stalc

Pay everyone a penny for correct answers.

The ABCs of Fun

A is for **ad-lib,** which fun teachers do.

B is for **balancing** the old and the new.

C is for **caring,** a heartfelt need.

D is for **discipline,** so Johnny can read.

E is for **engaging,** both heart and mind.

F is for **finding** time to unwind.

G is for **gallop,** technology's pace.

H is for **humor,** a saving grace

I is for **instilling** the highest ideal.

J is for **jokes** with positive appeal.

K is for **kindness** in all that you say.

L is for **laughter** to brighten the day.

M is for **mastery** in all that you do.

N is for **novelty** to uplift and renew.

O is for **outrageous** play that heals rifts.

P is for **positive** attitude shifts.

Q is for **quantum,** the leap we must take.

R is for **respect,** for self-esteem's sake.

S is for **smiling** and **spreading** good cheer.

T is for **teaching,** your choice of career.

U is for **unequaled,** which you will become.

V is for **variety** instead of humdrum.

W is for **warmth** and **wholesome** good fun.

X is for **"x-ample,"** when all's said and done.

Y is for **you,** for you are the gauge.

Z is for **zeal;** teach us well, humor sage.

18
Thanks to You

Most teachers spend years planting seeds and nurturing saplings, but never see the graceful oak trees that years later provide shade and protection for others. The following short story is about the human wish to see the fruits of one's labor. Although most teachers do not have the gratifying experience of receiving a thank-you letter fifteen years later, every committed, caring teacher deserves to receive one. This letter, then, is addressed to you.

Imagine it—it's Thanksgiving vacation. By some crazy quirk of fate and a few hours of unpaid overtime, you've no papers or tests to grade, no reports to submit, and no school board meetings to attend. No staff member has invited you to a wedding, baby shower, or housewarming party. For the first time, your time off is 100 percent yours. Your house is immaculate, the storm windows are up, the leaves are bagged your car has been winterized, and nothing is screaming at you for repair.

Your natural alarm clock wakes you promptly at 5:30 A.M. But today you roll over, smile, and fall back into a luxurious, deep sleep. You feel rested and refreshed when you awaken five hours later.

You putter around the kitchen for an hour and then sit down with last night's newspaper. Instead of skimming the headlines, you settle in with your liter of coffee and read the papers from the entire week. Next, you contemplate going to an afternoon matinee so you can buy a gargantuan tub of popcorn and an industrial-size soda. You recklessly decide to leave the rest of the day unplanned. It's now noon. You note how time flies when you're doing what comes naturally. At this rate, your vacation will be over before you can make the bed!

A sense of freedom propels you to empty the trash and take out the garbage without complaint. You walk to the front of your house to bring in the mail. Stuffed in your mailbox is a letter addressed to you, written in handwriting you don't recognize. The name on the return address seems vaguely familiar, so you read it several times, trying to match the name with a face. You dismiss permanent memory loss as the cause, simultaneously wondering if you've forgotten your key and accidentally locked yourself out of the house. You sit down, ignore the bills and holiday catalogs, and choose to read the letter first.

It is a thank-you letter from a student you taught over fifteen years ago! The letter contains a validation that you've always wished for but never believed you'd receive. You accepted that you probably would never see the fruits of your labor. You assumed that obscurity came with the territory—that teaching, although rewarding, was indeed a thankless job. Now, in your hand is proof that you made the right decision to become a teacher and that you have made a difference in someone's life.

You read the letter slowly, savoring every word, pausing only once to stifle an impulse to check it for spelling errors. . . .

Dear Teach,

You may not remember me, but I was the kid who nearly blew up your classroom with my volcano. I'll never forget the look on your face when I wheeled it in on my wagon. Most of my friends were making dioramas for their geography project, but I thought it would be neat to simulate a volcanic eruption. I think you knew I'd be the laughingstock of the class if we didn't at least try it out. Somehow you always knew the right thing to do, even when it might have been the wrong thing for you. I hope that makes sense to you. The volcano worked all right, remember? It worked way too well. I'm sorry if I got you in trouble – we didn't have to light it, really. But I was secretly glad that we did. I was the most popular kid in class from that moment on!

I never told you this, but all my projects were so big not because I wanted to show off, but because I was too hyperactive (you used to call me "energetic") to do tiny, detailed work. Do you remember that three people helped me to bring my model of the benzene ring to school, and when we unrolled my chart of the periodic table it was the size of two blackboards? You're probably glad I never tried to bake you a birthday cake!

I'll never forget the time you came to class dressed as Merlin the Magician to teach us about the solar system. You became so animated that your fake mustache flew off and landed on my head. We laughed so hard I fell onto the floor. I put the mustache on and imitated you (somewhat callously, as I recall), but it didn't phase you. You handed the hat to me, dubbed me Merlin of the Moment, and asked me if I had any information I wanted to share about the planets. I rattled off the distance of each planet from the sun, and you gave me the hat to keep. I still have it.

Thanksgiving is right around the corner, and every year I take a few moments to think about everything I'm thankful for. You introduced me to the giving of thanks, and it's been a tradition with me ever since. I thought it only right to give thanks to the person who had more faith in me than I had in myself.

Well, I am not a major success story. But I'm not a miserable failure either. I'm not the president of a bank, the drafter of bills, a nuclear physicist, a doctor, a lawyer, or an entrepreneur. I live a very modest life. But I'm happy. Truly happy. That wasn't always the case, as you may remember all too well.

I wanted to write to let you know that I'm okay and that if it weren't for you, well, who knows what might have happened. You taught me how to laugh at adversity; you actually showed me how to do it: "Place both your feet firmly on the ground, a shoulder's width apart, put both hands on your waist with your elbows out, and now lean back a little and laugh from deep within yourself, all the way down to your bones." I used to practice this in the mirror when I was home alone. I felt like I was rehearsing for The King and I.

> To be fond of something is better than merely to know it, and to find joy in it is better than merely to be fond of it.
> – Confucius

Thanks for never calling me slow, stupid, or impossible, or using me as an example of how not to act. I had more than enough of that at home! I think my family was doing the best they could; they just weren't aware of their cruelty. There's a label for it now – it's called a dysfunctional family. Thank you for creating a fully functional classroom! Thank you for allowing us to see you beyond your role, as a human being – full of contradictions, imperfections, and passion. You helped me to realize that I didn't have to be perfect. Even when you were angry with me, somehow I always knew that the boundaries you established for me were created to hold love in, not to keep it out.

> True humor springs not more from the head than from the heart; it is not contempt; its essence is love.
> – Thomas Carlyle

Looking back at it all, I must have driven you crazy! I guess I had to act that way so that I wouldn't drive myself crazy. I thank you for your patience and perseverance and for your insistence that I be myself.

Your loving pupil,
Merlin of the Moment

19
Song: "The Twelve Days of Classes"

This song is sung to the tune of "The Twelve Days of Christmas."

On the first day of classes, my teacher gave to me
The fun that learning can be.

On the second day of classes, my teacher gave to me
Two hemispheres,
And the fun that learning can be.

On the third day of classes, my teacher gave to me
Three play breaks,
Two hemispheres,
And the fun that learning can be.

On the fourth day of classes, my teacher gave to me
Four compliments,
Three play breaks,
Two hemispheres,
And the fun that learning can be.

On the fifth day of classes, my teacher gave to me
Discovery!
Four compliments,
Three play breaks,
Two hemispheres,
And the fun that learning can be.

On the sixth day of classes, my teacher gave to me
Sixth-sense awareness,
Flexibility!
Four compliments,
Three play breaks,
Two hemispheres,
And the fun that learning can be.

On the seventh day of classes, my teacher gave to me
Seven kinds of knowing,
Sixth-sense awareness,
Harmony!
Four compliments,
Three play breaks,
Two hemispheres,
And the fun that learning can be.

On the eighth day of classes, my teacher gave to me
Eight ways of caring,
Seven kinds of knowing,
Sixth-sense awareness,
Expectancy!
Four compliments,
Three play breaks,
Two hemispheres,
And the fun that learning can be.

On the ninth day of classes, my teacher gave to me
Nine energizers,
Eight ways of caring,
Seven kinds of knowing,
Sixth-sense awareness,
Spontaneity!
Four compliments,
Three play breaks,
Two hemispheres,
And the fun that learning can be.

On the tenth day of classes, my teacher gave to me
Ten relaxations,
Nine energizers,
Eight ways of caring,
Seven kinds of knowing,
Sixth-sense awareness,
Originality!
Four compliments,
Three play breaks,
Two hemispheres,
And the fun that learning can be.

On the eleventh day of classes, my teacher gave to me
Eleven laughing lessons,
Ten relaxations,
Nine energizers,
Eight ways of caring,
Seven kinds of knowing,
Sixth-sense awareness,
Generosity!
Four compliments,
Three play breaks,
Two hemispheres,
And the fun that learning can be.

On the twelfth day of classes, my teacher gave to me
Twelve master mind groups,
Eleven laughing lessons,
Ten relaxations,
Nine energizers,
Eight ways of caring,
Seven kinds of knowing,
Sixth-sense awareness,
Freedom to be me!
Four compliments,
Three play breaks,
Two hemispheres,
And the fun that learning can be.

Note: You can substitute any word you want or create a new word for the bold word for the fifth day. Other ideas include: Responsibility, Competency, Possibility, Rationality, "Jubilancy," Buoyancy, Sensitivity, Empathy, Diversity, Energy, Potentiality, Humanity, Bravery, Vitality, Clarity, Capability, Opportunity, and so forth.

20
Humor Homework

1. Recall one of the funniest moments you've had while teaching. Share it with your class.

2. Buy, borrow, or make three new props and surprise your students.

3. Write a love letter to a teacher you revered.

4. Dress out of character, and see how your class reacts.

5. Share with your class one of your more embarrassing moments. Have your students share some of theirs.

21

Play Sheet

1. List three ways that you can lighten up your classroom.

2. What unexpected or outrageous teaching methods have you used with success?

3. Identify other teachers who use humor in their classrooms. Observe them if possible, or share stories and ideas with them.

4. Write down as many ideas as you can about how you can influence other teachers to help them create a lighter atmosphere in their classrooms.

5. Generate a list of the positive and negative qualities of your school. List three ways you could help to turn the negative elements into positive ones.

22
Notes for Myself

Tons of Techniques

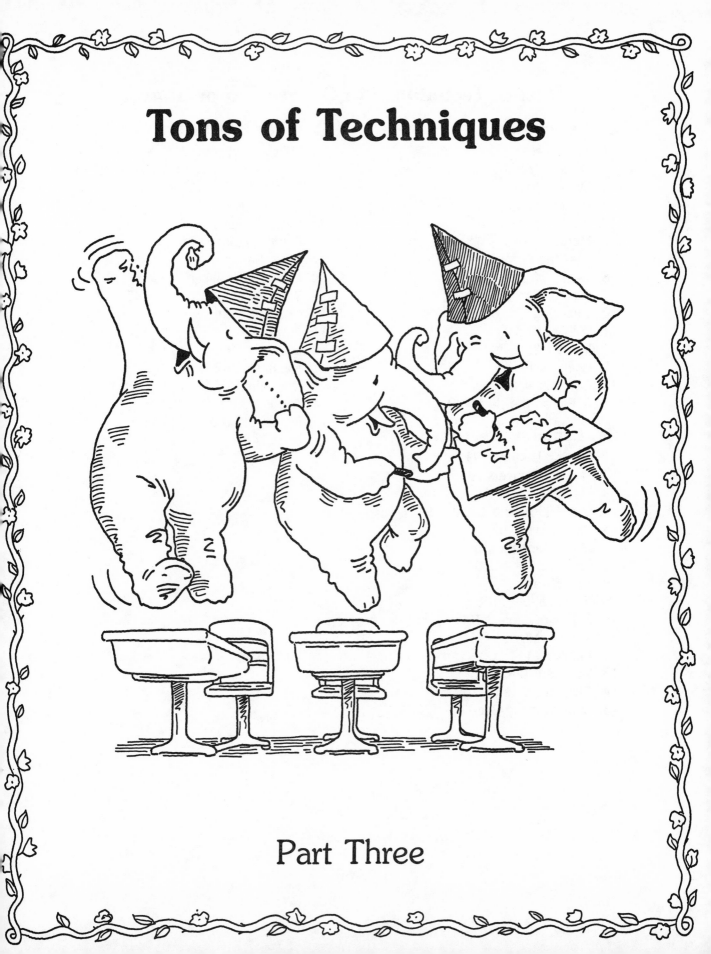

Part Three

List of Techniques in Order of Appearance

23. Warm-ups

1. Three Faces 68
2. Circle ZZZs 70
3. Switch-a-roo 72
4. Humorous Handshakes 74
5. "Daffy-nitions" 76
6. Mental Flossing 78
7. Pass the Compliment! 79
8. Wacky Wordies 81
9. Picking Grapes 82
10. Quacking Up 83
11. "Silly-ble" 84
12. Mirror 85
13. Chalk Walk 87
14. Commonalities 88
15. A Pat on the Back 90

24. Laughing Lessons

1. Singing Lessons 93
2. The Six Thinkers 95
3. Playful Review 97
4. Stack, Link, and Laugh! 99
5. Dr. Genius 102
6. Mind Mapping 103
7. Creative Debate 105
8. The Wizard 106
9. "Functuation" 108
10. Student Scholar 109
11. Moving Minds 111
12. Manikin 114
13. Tag-Team Talk 116
14. Gibberish Interpreter 118
15. Brainstorming Buddies 120

25. Play Breaks

1. Tongue Twisters 123
2. Sixty-Second "Mirth-Quake" 125
3. Classroom Storyteller 127
4. Conducting 128
5. Crazy Questions 130
6. Quote Quota 132
7. Brain Benders 133
8. Pass the Drawing! 135
9. What Are You Doing? 137
10. Count to Ten! 139
11. Transform the Object! 140
12. Let Your Fingers Do the Walking! 142
13. One-Minute Talk 143
14. The Forgetful Storyteller 144
15. Dream a Little Dream With Me! 146

23

Warm-ups

Higher education often overlooks the reality that the body and the brain are connected. For example, if you are in physical or emotional pain, it's difficult to concentrate and learn. Unfortunately, the older we get, the fewer opportunities we are given in school to move, stretch, and energize our bodies. When the body sits in one position for too long, the muscles stiffen or cramp. When the brain is focused for a long period, it, too, rebels. Without rest or a shift to a new activity, concentration diminishes and fatigue sets in. Students will learn more readily and retain information more effectively if time for physical activity is included prior to the lesson.

The purpose of the Warm-ups is to help students to lighten up, loosen up, and move into a state of positive expectancy. The following Warm-ups will open up the mind, relax the body, and create a receptive atmosphere. Each activity is designed to last two to three minutes, which is just enough time to create a relaxed learning environment

1. Three Faces

Overview

No matter what our age, we continue to delight in playful, harmless surprise. Have you ever been surprised by a call from a friend at the exact moment you were thinking of him or her? Have you spoken the same usual word or phrase aloud in unison with a friend? Human beings experience pleasure when a positive, playful, and unexpected moment occurs. In fact, a part of the brain thrives on the unexpected.

This Warm-up is based upon our love of surprises. The elements of imitation and intuition have been added. This exercise is adapted from an old game called "Rock, Paper, and Scissors," where the reward for winning the game was to hit the loser. The competitive elements have been deleted, and the elements that promote laughter, sharing, and caring remain. This game has been specifically adapted for use in the classroom and is based on a game created by Playfair.

Activity

[Say to students:] I'm going to make three faces, and I want you to follow me. The first face is a sad face, so let's make a sad expression together. What kind of gesture can we make with our hands and arms to show sadness? The second face is a mad expression, so let's furrow our brows, scrunch up our faces like a prune, and clench our fists. The third face is going to be a glad face, so make a big smile and put your

A smile confuses an
approaching frown.
– Anonymous

hands out in a gesture of happiness. Look glad. Do you remember what these three faces are? Let's try them again: sad, mad, and glad.

I'd like everyone in the room to find a partner. When everyone has a partner, stand back to back so that you can't see your partner's face. Now let's review the three faces one more time. Everyone make a sad face, now a mad face, and finally a glad face. I want you to pick one of these three faces—sad, mad, or glad. At the count of three, I'm going to ask all of you to turn around and show your partners which one of the three faces you picked. The idea is for you to match facial expressions with your partners without talking to them. Ready? One, two, three. Show your partners the facial expressions you chose.

How many of you had the same facial expression as your partner? Don't worry if you didn't, because you're going to get another chance to try to match expressions. Turn around again, and choose one of the three faces. You and your partner may choose different expressions this time if you want to. Remember, you are trying to match facial expressions with your partner, so you want to choose the facial expression that you think your partner is going to choose. Ready? One, two, three. Show your partner. How many of you matched the second time?

Variations

To encourage group cooperation, combine one set of partners with another set of partners, so they are in a group of four. Play the game as before, except the pairs discuss and then decide which facial expression they are going to show the other pair. You can then put the groups of four together with other groups of four and play the game again. Then continue to make larger groups until you have the class split in half with each half working as a team.

Have older students create three different movements and sound effects to go with the movements. This gives them control over the game. They'll feel more empowered when they match movements with each other. Allow one pair to teach their expressions and movements to the rest of the class and then lead the exercise. Make sure to remind them to create movements that they could show, *without embarrassment*, in front of their parents.

Sow a smile, and you'll reap a garden of delight.

2. Circle ZZZs

Overview

If a group grumbles and complains when you ask them to stand up, you can be assured that their bodies are fatigued and their brains are asleep as well. You can use this next exercise to shake up and wake up dozing minds and bodies. This Warm-up, unlike the arm circles that your gym teacher may have asked you to perform, is fun and energizing. The main objective of Circle ZZZs is to make use of physical exercise in a humorous way to give the group an outlet for their excess energy, reduce their stress, or get their blood circulating.

Activity

[Say to students:] Will everyone please stand up? Raise your arms as though you were making the letter "T," and give yourselves enough room so that you aren't touching anyone next to you. Good. Okay, you can put your arms down. Now, I'd like you to make a low-pitched ZZZ sound. It will sound as if millions of mosquitoes have filled this room. Lift your arms slightly, and rotate them in small circles while you are humming this sound. Now, slowly raise your arms, and at the same time make the circles larger. The ZZZ sound should become higher in pitch as you lift your arms over your heads. It will sound like electrical static. Good. And, now, you are going to reverse the process, by bringing your hands down and lowering your pitch until you are back in the beginning position.

Variations

Choose a student to lead the group through this activity, but ask the student to create a different movement and sound. You can use a variety of categories to get ideas for the sounds and movements. Ideas include sounds from these sources: mammals, birds, and mechanical or industrial noises. For movements, photographs, sculptures, abstract paintings, or postcards are possible inspirations.

Laughter helps us to turn and face in the same direction.

3. Switch-a-roo

Overview

How often do you give your students a series of directions (in five different ways) only to have students raise their hands and ask, "What are we supposed to do?" You'd like to ask them, "Where were you, out to lunch?" but instead, in your most composed voice, you ask, "Weren't you paying attention?"

Not paying attention is the worst blunder a student can commit because without the crucial ability to pay attention, very little learning occurs. Some students have developed an amazing capacity to shut out any incoming stimulus immediately upon walking into a classroom. The only activity capable of awakening them from their somnolent state is an unexpected fire drill. Admonishing students to "pay attention" will not only exhaust you, it will make the attention deficit students feel even more inadequate. A better solution is to give them the skills they need to improve their abilities.

Switch-a-roo is a playful way to encourage students to pay attention, to observe carefully, and to think creatively. This game was originally created by Matt Weinstein and Joel Goodman and can be found in their book *Playfair: Everybody's Guide to Noncompetitive Play.*

Activity

[Say to students:] Find a partner who is approximately your height, and stand directly in front of him or her. Determine who is taller—you or your partner. You should be about an arm and a half's length away from each other, so you can see your partner from head to toe. I'm going to give you exactly one minute to observe each other carefully, without talking. The idea is to observe each other without being critical or judgmental. Really concentrate on noticing everything you can

72

about your partners, such as what they're wearing, how they've parted their hair, and anything else you can see.

Now, stand back to back with your partners, so that your backs almost touch. I'm going to give you about two minutes, and in those two minutes I want you to change five things about your appearance. Maybe you want to roll up your sleeve or untie your shoe. I'm not going to give you any more suggestions because I want you to decide what to change, but you need to make five very different changes. Okay, you can start. [Allow one minute.] Is everyone done? Good.

Now when I tell you, you'll both turn around and look at each other again. What I want you to do is try to guess what changes your partners have made. The taller person is going to guess first, and then the other partner will guess the changes. See if you can guess all five changes. But before I have you turn around, I want to say one very important thing: After you have guessed these changes, stay with these changes. Don't touch them, or go back to the way you looked. You'll see why in a moment. Okay, you can turn around and look. Remember, the taller person starts to guess first, and then you switch. [Allow about one minute.] Great. Did everyone guess? If not, you can tell your partners what they missed.

Now, turn back to back again. I hope that you stayed with your original changes, because I am now going to ask you to change five new things about your appearance. Notice I said five *new* things, because you can't change or alter anything that you've already changed. When I tell you to turn around, you'll try to guess the new changes. Everyone ready? Okay, turn around and guess those five new changes. [If they complain because they think that they can't find any more things to change, use this as a springboard to talk about how easily we give up when faced with challenges. Brainstorm about how they could creatively solve the problem (for example, switching clothing with someone nearby, changing postures or facial expressions, leaving the room, and so forth).]

Variations

A shorter variation of Switch-a-roo is to have the class observe one student for thirty seconds. Then send that student out of the room with a card that instructs him or her to change five things about his or her appearance. You can write several suggestions on the card (untie your shoe, roll up a pant leg, and so forth) so that he or she gets the idea. When he or she comes back in, have the class guess the changes. You can do this several times with different students. By the second student, they will be better observers. You can use this activity to talk about the importance of paying attention the first time, because often during the school day they may not have a second chance and may miss the opportunity to learn.

4. Humorous Handshakes

Overview

To protect both teacher and student alike, touch has been, for all practical purposes, removed from the learning environment. Unfortunately, because of the fear of lawsuits, teachers have to be very careful about how to use touch. In our fear, we have banned touch as a form of communication. Even the reassuring hand on the shoulder might be suspect.

Research shows that the less we touch, the more "out of touch" we become with one another. Inappropriate touch often comes from not knowing how to touch and be touched in nurturing and nonsexual ways. The two main forms of touch modeled on television are violence and seduction. We are fast becoming a touched-starved culture, and consequently we are losing our ability to relate to others in healthy ways.

The Humorous Handshake Warm-up gives students the opportunity to connect physically with one another using handshakes. Because the handshakes are playful and funny, any embarrassment or awkwardness about touching is circumvented. The benefit derived from this game comes not only from the laughter, but from the sensation of touch. Students who playfully shake hands will be less likely to fight with one another. To reduce self-consciousness, don't mention that touch is included as part of the experience.

Activity

[Say to students:] I'd like to explore the ways people greet one another. What's one way that you have seen? [Wait for a handshake.] I need two volunteers to come up to the front to demonstrate what a typical American handshake looks like. Who has seen a different kind of handshake? Why don't you pick a partner and come up and demonstrate it. [Have students demonstrate various handshakes.]

What we're going to do is create
a humorous handshake to use in our
classroom. It will be our way to greet
one another. First, I want you to find
a partner. Good. I'm going to give
you three minutes to create a new
and outrageous handshake for us. It
has to be simple enough that we will

remember it, but creative enough to be fun and enjoyable. You can combine elements of other handshakes that you've seen and add a new twist to them, or you can come up with something original. I'm going to write your names on a sheet of paper. We'll draw two names out of a hat to see which two lucky people get to create the humorous handshake for the week.

I may take the opportunity sometime during the week to call out "Humorous Handshake," and you'll have exactly thirty seconds to give the handshake to as many people as you can. You might want to practice it a few times with your classmates, just to make sure that you know it and can repeat it upon command.

5. "Daffy-nitions"

Overview

Have you ever noticed how much young children love to rearrange the sound of words, interchange syllables, and create new words? This is the creative genius within doing its daily workout. As we become more and more immersed in left-brain activities, we begin to lose the wonderful skill of taking the mundane and twisting it around just enough to make it more interesting. This Warm-up will help students to revert playfully to a skill that was once an enjoyable pastime. "Daffy-nitions" are zany new words that students create and then define. Here are some examples: Braino—a clear liquid that is used to unclog rusty mental pipes before a test review; Tupperware Brain Syndrome—the peculiar syndrome that occurs when nothing goes in the brain or nothing comes out and the only stimulation the brain gets is when it's occasionally burped to remove the stale air! This is a great exercise to help students develop creative thinking skills and a sense of humor.

It takes a long time to become young.
– Pablo Picasso

Activity

[Say to students:] Okay, I'd like all of you to pair off with a partner and make sure that both of you have a paper and a pen or pencil. We're going to create some "daffy-nitions" today. They are creative syllables or words that you put together to invent a new word or a new phrase. If, for example, our theme were memory, you could create the word "memori-gram," which is a medical test to check up on the health and well-being of your memory. You're advised to take a "memori-gram" as soon as you reach the age of thirty-five, if you remember. Does everybody get the idea? Are there any questions so far? Great. Our theme for today is going to be [insert theme]. You'll have one minute to brain-

76

storm and write down any ideas that come to mind. You'll have two minutes to see if you can come up with a few new "daffy-nitions" that relate to our theme word. Get ready. . . . Get set. . . . Get smarted!

Variations

To generate more ideas, have students pair off in groups of four or six. We have successfully done this activity with an entire class. Two people write all of the idea words on the board, while the teacher and other students brainstorm. Or you can do this as a free-flow activity without having a particular theme.

Laughter: the fixer, the mixer, the great elixir.

6. Mental Flossing

Overview

Most cultures throughout history have created rituals for a number of events that hold deep meaning for them, despite how strange they may appear to an outsider. Building upon the "daffy-nitions" theme, the ridiculous ritual of mental flossing may be performed in unison by any size group. The benefits include physical exercise, humor, and the mysterious bonding that seems to occur "whenever two or more of you are gathered in this game."

Activity

[Say to students:] I'd like everyone to stand up and take a moment to stretch before we perform a special ritual that will help us to clear any of the flack that may be stuck in the crevices of our minds. That's right, stretch all of those muscles, including the brain biceps! Now, stand with your feet slightly apart and hold each hand about six inches from each ear. Imagine that you are holding a piece of string in each hand. Good! Now, begin to move that string back and forth horizontally from side to side. Take a moment to look around, and you will see that everyone is doing this together. Now, let's take a moment to do this in sync. Are you ready? One, two. One, two. One, two. In, out. In, out. Great! So, if you did know what you were doing, what would the answer be? You've got it! You are mental flossing. We are doing this to prevent truth decay. You see, the truth is that you are all potential geniuses. And now that we have flossed, we are ready for another learning adventure.

Variations

Have students come up with other ridiculous classroom rituals that include body movements, such as a ritual for remembering all of the answers on the test, a ritual for silencing a loud room, a ritual for waking everybody up on a tough day, or even a ritual for announcing a Warm-up or Play Break.

7. Pass the Compliment!

Overview

Can you imagine what would occur in the future if all gatherings conducted by the United Nations started out with three compliments given to each nation attending? It's a little hard to imagine, which is why this exercise was created. Based on the old "Pass the Whisper" game, this activity is fun and energizing, while slipping in the soothing strokes that will act as a salve for students.

Activity

[Say to students:] How many of you remember playing the game "Pass the Whisper"? It is also called the "Telephone Game." Well, for those of you who aren't sure, it is a listening game. We are going to play a special version of it today called "Pass the Compliment." Please stand up and begin to think of a complimentary word that you would like to give to the person behind you. Use a word that compliments the person's character, such as *friendly, clever,* or *kind,* rather than one that compliments the person's appearance, such as *slim, handsome,* or *attractive.* If you don't know the person behind you, imagine that you are giving the person this compliment as a gift. Wouldn't it be great if we could give people a positive quality just by whispering it in their ears? Well, who's to say we can't?

Laughter is the shortest distance between two people. – Victor Borge

Does everybody have a word? We are going to do this by rows. We'll start with the head of the row. Please turn to the person behind you and whisper, "I want you to know that I think that you are . . . " For example, you might use the word *incredible.* Then whisper your compliment.

The next person will whisper, "I want you to know that I think that you are *incredible* and *fabulous.*" The third person must remember the first two compliments and add a third, and so on all the way down the row. The last person in the row must say the entire complimentary sentence aloud! [The row then checks to see if each student heard the compliments accurately.]

I think you are very brave.

Variations

Pick one student at the end of each day and have his or her classmates give that student a compliment. Or take a compliment break in which students give group compliments randomly, such as, "We're great teamworkers!" or "We're good and getting better all the time!" Or start an "I'm great because . . ." sheet of paper going around the room. When the last person has added his or her comments, read the entire list back to the class.

Instead of compliments, have a student in the first row make a funny face. When the student has made a face that he or she can maintain, the student turns around and shows it to the next person. Encourage students not to laugh or lose their concentration. The student who is passing the "funny face" holds the pose until the student who is receiving the face can imitate it. Once the second student has mirrored the first student's funny face as closely as possible, that student makes a different facial expression. He or she then turns around and passes the new face to the next person. This continues until everyone has had a chance to imitate a face and make up a new one. We promise that this game will produce many laughs.

Every joy is gain, and gain is gain, however small. — Robert Browning

8. Wacky Wordies

Overview

Is a picture really worth a thousand words? What about a picture that includes words? Wacky Wordies are a wonderful way to whet one's whimsical whistle! They also exercise both sides of the brain simultaneously, since this Warm-up involves looking at pictures while interpreting them. Wacky Wordies are a hit with all ages.

Activity

[Say to students:] We are now going to try a Warm-up called Wacky Wordies. You'll notice there are some examples on the board. To find the hidden phrase, you look at the picture, read the words, and then see if you can put them together to create a meaningful saying. Let's try the first one together. ["Circles under the eyes."] If you know the answer, please remain silent so that everyone gets a chance to guess. [Take about thirty seconds before moving on.] How many people think they have found the answer? You'll have another opportunity to guess when we look at the other nine Wacky Wordies. "Circles under the eyes" is the correct answer. Did anyone come up with another answer? We are usually taught to look for one right answer, but I want you to know that right now it's okay to come up with more than one right answer. Now, you'll have a few more minutes to look over the other examples.

i i i i o o o o	sight love sight sight	O V A T I O N	. that's	shape or	ship

often
   not
often
   not
often
	sitting
	world
		[income]	hand
			hand
			hand
			deck
				W
				A
				L
				K
				G N I	

See page 147 for answers.

Variations

Have students break into small groups and brainstorm well-known phrases and sayings. After coming up with a list, give them time to create their own Wacky Wordies. Use them in future Warm-ups or ask your students to drop new ideas for Wacky Wordies into a special box labeled "WACKBOX."

9. Picking Grapes

Overview

Have you ever noticed how well most mammals can stretch? They stretch every muscle and appear thoroughly relaxed afterward. Although humans are considered the most intelligent of mammals (using human criteria, of course), it would be to our benefit to learn a few small tricks from our fellow creatures. Brain research has proved that a calm mind and a relaxed body bring about an alert brain. This Warm-up is designed to have students stretching and breathing deeply while participating creatively in a humorous exercise.

Activity

[We recommend that you read this activity and demonstrate the activity to the class before leading them through it as a group.]

[Say to students:] We're going to take a few minutes to calm our minds and stretch our bodies so that our brains will be in full gear. Let's all stand up for a moment and free our hands so that we can pick grapes. Now, imagine that there are luscious grapes on a vine that is just out of reach. Watch as I show you how to pick them. Look up and to your right. With your right arm, stretch as far as you can to get that big grape, while taking a short inhalation at the same time. Oh, don't forget to pick two more grapes! Reach for the second with your left arm, and take another short inhalation. Now, pick the third grape with your right arm while taking a third inhalation. Great! (Grape!)

Now, bend over and drop the three grapes into a small bucket near your feet. Slowly exhale as you do this. Ahhh . . . that's right! Reach up to your left, and you'll see three more delicious grapes. Starting with the right arm, pick another large grape while breathing in. Now, pick another grape with your left arm, and really s-t-r-e-t-c-h that arm. Finally, pick a third grape with your right arm while breathing in. As you drop the grapes into the bucket, slowly exhale once more.

And, now, you'll see a few more grapes on the vine. Pick three more, and then drop them into the bucket. Really stretch your arms as you breathe in. Great! I know that some of you would like to go on, but I'm afraid that this might lead to some "wine-ing." You can have a seat as soon as you eat those well-earned grapes that you picked! [Pick other kinds of fruits or pass around a bowl of real grapes at the end of this activity.]

10. Quacking Up

Overview

Movement, sound, and humor combine to create this energizing Warm-up that will have everybody laughing and bonding as students search with their eyes closed for all the "animals" in their group.

Activity

[Say to students:] Today, I'll be whispering animal names to the first one in each row. [Whisper an animal name to the student at the head of each row. Choose animals that make sounds that are easy to mimic, such as ducks, dogs, cats, horses, sheep, cows, owls, wolves, and so forth.] Now I'd like you to whisper the name of that animal to each person in your row, from front to back. Okay, do you all know what animals you are? We are going to stand and form a tight circle. Now, close your eyes. In a moment, I'll ask you to make your animal sound out loud. The purpose of this Warm-up is to see how many of you can find the other animals like you within three minutes.

With your eyes shut, walk around, and as soon as you hear the same animal's sound, join hands with the person making the sound. Continue to make your sound while searching for the rest of your group. At the end of the search, we'll see which group is largest. Are you ready? Eyes shut? Begin! Remember to keep shuffling around and keep your eyes shut. Rely on your sense of hearing, and listen for that lost sheep, wolf, or cow.

Variations

As your students file into class, either whisper the animal names to them or hand them slips of paper with the names of their animals on them. Another possibility is to have a student walk around and whisper an animal's name in each student's ear. Use about seven different animals. For a more advanced variation, have students pick their animal sounds, and see how many other students picked the same sound at the end of two minutes.

11. "Silly-ble"

Overview

Students often have a larger vocabulary and a better grasp of the English language than they realize. This game serves two functions. It excites students about their potential to use words creatively, and it challenges them to think and write at a higher, more complex level. They will learn that wordplay can be fun and entertaining rather than intimidating. It's also a great way to help them to warm up and wake up for any writing, poetry, or communication unit you'll be doing.

Activity

[Have students take out a sheet of paper and a pencil, and number the paper from one to ten.]

[Say to students:] I'm going to give you exactly two minutes. In those two minutes, I want you to think of words that begin with the letter "I" that have four or more syllables. [Adjust the number of syllables for your grade level.] An example of an "I" word is the word *interesting*. Try to make a list of ten or more words. The person who reaches ten words first, raise your hand. Don't worry about the spelling right now. [When the first student gets ten, you can go on to the next part of the game.]

Now, I'm going to prove to you that you know more words than you think. I'm going to ask the first person in the row to tell me one of his or her four-syllable words. If you do not have that word written on your sheet of paper, add it to your list. I'm going to ask everyone for a word, so when we're through, you should have over twenty words on your paper. I'm sure as soon as you hear another four-syllable "I" word, you're going to say, "Hey, I knew that word. Why didn't I think of it?"

Variations

Now that your students have a list of twenty words, they can use those words to create an improvisational story. This can be done verbally or as a writing exercise. For example, if the words from the first four students were *interesting, intestinal, impossible,* and *identify,* the first student would begin a story using his or her word, the second student would have to add to the story and include his or her word, and so forth. The story might sound like this. First student: "It was late at night. I was studying a very *interesting . . .*" Second student: " . . . book about *intestinal* problems." Third student: "Unfortunately, the vocabulary was *impossible* to understand." Fourth student: "I had to *identify* every part of the intestine."

Once the students trust that they know more than monosyllabic words, you can begin to have even more fun playing with words. This variation combines the ideas from "Silly-ble" with the ideas from "Daffy-nitions." A great verbal Warm-up, it takes a minute or two and can be done in rows. Ask the first student in a row to think of a word that has more than one syllable. He or she will say only the first syllable aloud. The second student adds the second syllable; the third student, the third syllable and so forth until you have created a new word. Then have the students define it. Start another word until everyone has had a chance to play.

12. Mirror

Overview

Many of us travel through life oblivious to the details and beauty of our surroundings. We don't notice the new haircuts of our closest friends; we can't give directions to a stranger; or we don't remember the color of the house across the street from us even though we see it every day. As we learn the art of concentration and focus, we can sensitize ourselves and become richer in the process. This is a game of observation, attention, and concentration. It's often used in theater training to help actors become aware of the subtle nuances of gesture so that they can create believable characters.

This game is also a great way to provoke discussions about the differences between observing others to understand and empathize with them or to ridicule and ostracize them.

Activity

[Because choosing a partner can sometimes be awkward, it's best to have an arbitrary method for students to use.]

[Say to students:] I'd like you to hop either on your left foot or your right foot. Now, hop over to one other person who is hopping on the same foot as you are, and when you find that person you can stop hopping. That person is now your partner for this next exercise.

Determine who is the taller between the two of you. Please move about the length of an arm and a half away from each other. The taller person is going to be the "Mover," and the shorter person is going to be the "Mirror." Movers, I want you to begin moving your right arms in slow motion. Mirrors, if you were looking into a mirror and you wanted to follow the motions of your partner, which hand would you move? Your left hand! Good. I want you to follow the person who is moving as closely as you can. Move as though you are your partner's mirror. Movers, keep your movements slow. The idea is to work with your partner as closely as possible. If you start to laugh, look at your partner's forehead instead of your partner's eyes.

Now, Movers, I want you to start moving your left arm in slow motion. Mirrors, try to follow them. Okay. Now you have the idea. Movers, you can move any body part you want. For example, try bending, twisting, and lifting your shoulders.

Experiment. Make faces into the mirror—but slowly, so your partner can follow you. Movers, try moving a few steps backward or to the side. Keep your eyes on each other. Try balancing in odd positions. Good. Now switch. Movers, now become the Mirrors for your partners, and Mirrors become the Movers. [Talk the students through it step by step. Remind them to move in slow motion. You also can suggest activities for the Movers to do, such as brushing their teeth or hair, tying their shoes, miming a sport, and so on.]

Variations

You can choose one person to be the "Mover of the Day." The Mover takes the lead during the times you designate. For example: "In a moment, I'd like you to take out your math book and turn to page 21, but you are going to follow the Mover to do it." Or, "I'd like the Mover to erase the blackboard and everyone will follow him/her." Everyone then knows to move in slow motion, imitating the Mover. You could also have the Mover stand in front of the class and lead the movements for a minute or two. This way, everyone is moving together, mirroring the person in the front.

> It is only in sorrow bad weather masters us; In joy we face the storm and defy it. – Amelia Barr

A longer variation of Mirror is to work with a group of six to eight students at a time. The eight students form a circle, and a student from the remaining (seated) group is sent out of the room. The group chooses a leader who initiates the movement, and they begin moving together in slow motion, always following the designated Mover's lead. The person who was sent out of the room then enters the center of the circle and tries to guess who is leading the motions. He or she is allowed three guesses. If he or she can't guess, a new student is sent out of the room, and the process begins again. This exercise helps build cooperation, because the objective of the group is to work so well together that the person entering can't tell who is leading or who is following.

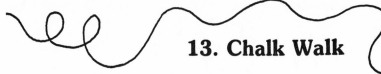

13. Chalk Walk

Overview

No matter what the age, students enjoy writing on the blackboard. Often students will write on the board when you're not looking. This Warm-up allows them to use the blackboard "legally" in a fun and playful manner. It's fun to divide students into three teams and send one student from each team up to the board to try to draw an object that's whispered to him or her. This "Racing and Erasing" game is an old favorite! No wonder the commercial games "Pictionary" and "Win, Lose, or Draw" are so successful. Chalk Walk is less frenetic, but still highly creative. The students get a chance to create a collaborative drawing without pressure, because it will be erased once it's finished. This game helps prepare students for working on other cooperative projects, such as murals or group presentations.

Activity

[Make sure to have different colors and widths of chalk available.]

[Say to students:] Today, we're going to go on a Chalk Walk. Who wants to start? Come on up and choose a piece of chalk. I'd like you to start drawing a line on the board. There's only one rule: The chalk cannot leave the board. Once you pick the chalk up from the board, that's the signal that you're done. There is a time limit of ten seconds, although if it takes you less time, that's perfectly acceptable. Each person will get a chance to add to your line drawing. We'll move down the rows. The idea is to work quickly, without judging your work, because it will be erased shortly after the last person has had a chance. You can add shading, you can overlap the lines, and you can do anything you feel adds to this creation as long as you don't lift the chalk off the board.

Variations

You can hang a large sheet of butcher paper across the board and use magic markers instead. This could be a project that you add to over a longer period. If you are working on a larger, more permanent piece, make sure everyone gets to sign it when it's finished.

The more you play this game, the more sophisticated you can become with it. You can set parameters, such as draw only circles, no line should touch any other line, draw an outdoor scene, draw with your weaker/nonwriting hand, and so forth. Ask the students to suggest variations.

87

14. Commonalities

Overview

Students need to learn to celebrate and appreciate individual differences. But they also need to discover the things that they have in common. This exercise is a very quick method of helping students to find similarities and share them with one another. It's much easier to resolve conflicts when you know there are many things you have in common. This Warm-up helps students to see one another as human beings instead of as stereotypes.

Activity

[Say to students:] I'd like you to find two other people who are wearing at least one color of clothing that is the same as a color you are wearing. These two people must be people you do not know very well. You will then form groups of three. Please find some space in the room, and, then, as a threesome, squat down. Don't sit; squat.

You will have exactly two minutes to talk as fast as you possibly can. What you are going to talk about is yourself. Your goal is to find one thing that the three of you share in common. Maybe you've traveled out of state, maybe everyone likes cold pizza for breakfast. It doesn't matter what it is, as long as the three of you share it.

When you find something in common, you are going to be so excited that you'll leap, and I mean *leap*, to your feet and shout the number "One!" with as much enthusiasm as you can muster. Then return to the squatting position, and keep talking until you find a second thing in common. Then leap to your feet and shout out the number "Two!" The idea is for the three of you to find ten things that you have in common, within two minutes.

Now, I know how creative you are! You're already thinking of things like "Are we cool? Yeah, we're cool. *One!*" "Do you cut your fingernails? Yup. *Two!*" "Do you speak English? Yeah. *Three!*" This is cheating. Your goal is to discover obscure and unusual facts about one another. Facts such as: "My brother rides a unicycle." "Really? My mom does, too." "I ride one, too." "*One!*" Don't go for the obvious. Dig a little deeper. Ask strange and wonderful questions. Ready . . . *Go!*

Variations

A standard variation of this game is called the "Scavenger Hunt." First you gather unusual information about your students. Don't let them know why you are collecting this information. You then create a series of statements that reflect what you've learned. Write these statements on a sheet of paper, making sure to leave enough room for a student's signature or initials. (There should be one statement per student.) Make enough copies of the statement sheet for all your students. Sample statements include: Find someone who has six older brothers; find someone who has had his or her tonsils removed; and so forth.

Give the class a time limit and rules for the game. The objective is for all the students to match a person with each statement. When they have found a match, they then ask the student to write his or her name next to the statement. The first student who has a signature for each statement is the winner. You can create rules, such as: You can only ask the same person two questions, or the first person to come up with ten matches is the winner. At the end of the game, you can read off each statement and ask the students to stand if a statement is true for them.

15. A Pat on the Back

Overview

Unfortunately, many students can more easily list their faults than they can list their talents. Studies have shown that self-esteem is closely tied to success and the ability to be motivated positively. Some students compensate for their low sense of self-esteem by constantly "bragging" about themselves. This kind of bragging is often a cover-up for deeply felt inadequacies. Bragging has a basis in comparison and usually manifests itself as one-upmanship. Students who are confident and secure rarely need to brag, feel superior, gloat, or put others down to feel positive about themselves.

It's crucial to counteract the many negative messages that students either tell themselves or are told by their significant others (messages such as "You can't . . . you'll never . . . why try?"). This Warm-up shows students how to give themselves positive messages without comparing themselves to others.

Activity

[Say to students:] Will those of you who like chocolate ice cream raise your right arm in the air and make the letter "C" with your hand? Those of you who like vanilla ice cream better than chocolate, will you raise your left arm in the air and make the letter "V" with your hand? I'd like you to find one other person who likes a different flavor than you like, so if you like chocolate, you want to find someone who likes vanilla. That person will be your partner for the next exercise.

The person who likes vanilla is going to begin. I'm going to give you thirty seconds. In those thirty seconds, you are going to tell the absolute truth about yourself to your partner. You are

going to tell your partner absolutely everything that you like about yourself. This includes things that deserve a pat on the back, things that you're good at doing, or positive character traits. Mention *anything* wonderful that you can think of. You are going to try to say one thing every few seconds so that you have mentioned several things at the end of thirty seconds. Of course, you are going to be concentrating so hard that you might forget to count. This is where your partners are going to help you. Your partners are going to count aloud as you list what you love about yourself. They are not going to snicker or make faces if you say something like "I am an extremely intelligent person." Instead, they are going to support you one hundred percent, no matter what you say. After all, your partners will need your support when they list what they like about themselves.

If all your thoughts about yourself are negative, try verbal aikido by asserting the opposite! This is called an affirmation, which is a truth told in advance—it just hasn't happened *yet*! So if you don't like your body, instead say, "I love my body" or "I have a healthy body." Your partner will never know you are stretching the truth. You have thirty seconds. Are you ready? Go for it. [Give the chocolates a chance to do the exercise.]

If you had difficulty with this exercise, tell yourself, "I love myself. I love myself. I love myself." Any time you notice that you are putting yourself down or thinking horrible thoughts about who you are, remind yourself that you are getting better all the time and you don't have to be perfect.

Variations

You can take time during class to ask if some students have something they would like to share that deserves a pat on the back. No accomplishment is too small. The class can help you create appropriate verbal responses, such as "Ooooh . . . ahhhh," "Good going!" and so forth. It's important to spend time talking about the importance of real support and encouragement. Otherwise, you run the risk of having this activity turn into a vehicle for ridicule.

24
Laughing Lessons

Laughing Lessons are designed to incorporate humor and play into your teaching curriculum. The following ideas can be adapted to suit any subject matter and work with any age group. These Laughing Lessons can last from five minutes to forty-five minutes. Read through the activities, and watch your students' mental gears begin to turn.

Remember, the key word for an innovative educator is *adapt*, rather than *adopt*. As you page through the Warm-ups and the Play Breaks, be on the lookout for those techniques you might be able to adapt to fit into your curriculum or turn into a Laughing Lesson. If you occasionally pause and ask yourself, "Are we having fun yet?" and you get a string of "No, no, never, never," you might want to try a few of these lessons.

1. Singing Lessons

Overview

The advertising industry has long paired information with music. This unbeatable combination guarantees that unsuspecting listeners will remember what they hear. But education, still gnawing on the dinosaur artifacts of traditional learning models, has not yet taken advantage of the impact that learning through song can provide. This Laughing Lesson gives you the opportunity to capitalize on what advertisers have known for years. This is an enlivening addition to any lesson plan.

Activity

[The example given here is taken from an English literature course.]

[Say to students:] As you know, we are going to be studying a unit on Emily Dickinson. To bring her writing to life and appreciate its subtleties, we are going to take a creative approach. We are going to create a song about her. Today, I'll divide you into brainstorming groups. Each group will be in charge of creating a song that can be sung to a familiar tune. After you have had a chance to practice it, you teach it to the rest of us. Sounds like fun, doesn't it?

You'll find that the words will be picked up easily by your classmates because they already know the song. You're going to have a lot of fun with this! Before I ask you to get into groups, I am going to teach you a little song that will give you some facts about Emily's life. I have put the words to the tune of "Yankee Doodle Went to Town," so I know that you will pick it up very easily. Let's look at the words and read them aloud before we sing the song. [Have the words on the board or on a handout for each student.] Great! Now let's sing the song together:

Emily Dickinson was a poet
Born in Massachusetts.
She kept her poems in a trunk
And hardly ever used them.
Emily Dickinson, keep it up,
Keep the poetry going.
One fine day, they all will see,
Your inner genius flowing.

Variations

This exercise can be adapted to any subject matter for instructional or review purposes and always raises the enthusiasm level.

2. The Six Thinkers

Overview

The Six Thinkers exercise has been adapted from Dr. Edward deBono's Six Thinking Hats exercise. Many of us see the world through rose-, green-, or gray-colored glasses. The way we approach the world is based on our personal "thinking style." If we are optimistic, we look for solutions. If we are creative, we usually look for a new approach. If we are pessimistic, we look for the problems. This exercise is an excellent way to offer students an opportunity to try on many different perspectives and look objectively at the many different sides of an issue. It can be adapted to any subject matter.

Activity

[You will need to find or make six hats for this exercise. They can be made from paper. You'll need the colors blue, green, yellow, white, red, and gray.]

[Say to students:] Today we are going to approach our discussion in a new way. You will try on several different perspectives by playing a game called "The Six Thinkers." Because we are discussing [fill in the subject matter], our Six Thinkers will do the same. [At this point, select six students from the group to become the Six Thinkers.]

I am going to ask our Six Thinkers to come to the front of the room and each select and wear one of the six hats on the desk. Then please stand in a row facing the class. Okay, now that we have our Six Thinkers in proper garb, let me introduce them to you:

1. **Blue Hat: The Controller.** Starts each sentence crossing the arms and saying, "We must control . . . " Let's all say this aloud. Good.
2. **Green Hat: The Creator.** Starts each sentence pointing a forefinger to the temple and saying, "Aha! I've got it . . . " Let's say this together. That's it!
3. **Yellow Hat: The Optimist.** Starts each sentence with palms up and saying, "Let's look at the bright side . . . " Let's say it aloud. Great!
4. **White Hat: The Objective Thinker.** Starts each sentence with a forefinger pointing and saying, "Let's look at the facts . . . " Let's say this statement, too. Good job!
5. **Red Hat: The Feeler.** Starts each sentence with a hand over the heart area and saying, "What I feel is . . . " Let's try it aloud. Okay.
6. **Gray Hat: The Pessimist.** Starts each sentence shaking the head no and saying, "No, no, no . . . " Let's practice this last one. That's it.

[Have everyone practice the opening statements and motions together, even if the Six Thinkers will be the only ones speaking.]

Okay, now that we understand who is who, we are going to have a discussion about [fill in the subject matter]. Six Thinkers, your goal will be to answer my question in character. You will not be forced to answer. Answer only if you have an "urge." If the hat you are wearing does not represent your true perspective, all the better. We want to look at this issue from as many different perspectives as possible. Let's begin.

Variations

This can be handled in several ways. The thinkers themselves can carry on a lively and controversial conversation as the rest of the class listens. Or students can ask any thinker for his or her opinion or perspective on a certain matter. The thinkers can be divided into two teams for a lively debate. Or the six hats can be left up on the desk, and students can file up one at a time, put on a hat, and express an opinion about the matter under discussion. This is an excellent activity that evokes stimulating and thought-provoking comments. It's also very entertaining. You'll be surprised by the risks people are willing to take when they have been given permission to be "in character."

Real joy, believe me, is a serious matter.
– Seneca

3. Playful Review

Overview

Madeline Hunter was not the first educator to make *review* a household word for educators. Brain research in recent years has also shown that the brain benefits from the frequent review of subject matter. In fact, frequent review im-

proves retention as well. This Laughing Lesson adds a playful touch to the review process, making it an instant classroom favorite with all age groups.

Activity

[You will need a large ball for this exercise. We recommend a blowup ball, a pillow ball, or a light-weight plastic ball.]

[Say to students:] Today, we are going to review in a playful new way. Will everyone please stand in a tight circle? Imagine that the ball that I have in my hand is a *magic ball*. It holds the answers to all the material that we have been studying recently. When I ask you a review question, if you think you know the answer, you can hold out your hands. Then, when I throw the ball to you, you answer the question.

If, for some reason, the answer that you give me does not match the question that I have asked, you can throw the ball to someone who has a question that fits your answer. We do this so that you won't feel self-conscious if you give an answer other than the one that I am looking for. We also do this so that you realize that this exercise is intended to be fun!

If you answer correctly, then you get to ask the next question and throw the ball to someone who wants to answer it. What happens if you can't think of a question after you have answered one? Then you can simply ask, "Who would like to catch this ball and ask the next review question?"

Does everybody follow me so far? Great. Let's do a trial run. [Shape your questions to fit your subject matter. Give your students some examples modeled on the example here.]

"I have the ball in my hand, and my question is: What is the definition of *phosphorescent*?"

"[Carl] has his hands outstretched, so I'll throw the ball to him. What is your answer?"

[Carl] catches the ball and says, "A crescent shape on a piece of phosphorus."

"Well, not exactly. Can someone create a question that fits the answer that [Carl] just gave?"

[Mary] catches the ball and says, "What is a 'phoon'?" [Laughter.]

"Yes, that question will work! Now, [Mary], do you know the answer to my question?"

[Mary] answers, "Yes, *phosphorescent* means 'continuing to shine in the dark after exposure to light.'"

"That answer fits. Now it's your turn to ask the group another question."

Okay, if everyone understands how this game works, we'll get started. Remember, the only person who answers aloud is the person who catches the ball. Please throw the ball only to those who signal that they would like to catch it! We'll do this for about five minutes.

[We suggest that you use this game to review fifteen to twenty concepts learned within the past two to three classes. More than this puts students on overload. If you'd like to throw in a few nonsense questions for effect, it will lighten the mood.]

Variations

Have students get into groups of about eight and play the review game in their small groups. You can use potatoes, rubber balls, or bean bags, for example. Or, as the instructor, you can walk up and down the aisles asking one question at a time and throwing the object to students for the answer. After the question is answered, the ball is thrown back to you. This way, you can be in charge of asking the questions. Although it saves time, it's not as participatory.

We must laugh before we are happy, for fear we die before we laugh at all.   – La Bruyère

4. Stack, Link, and Laugh!

Overview

Nothing triggers memory quite the way nonsense and humor do. One of the chief principles of mnemonics (rules for assisting memory) is that the more outrageous the images, the easier the information is to recall. This Laughing Lesson is a terrific way to create a memorable learning experience and to tap into the creativity and humor of your students. Its benefits will be reflected in higher test scores, plus it will be lots of fun!

Activity

[Say to students:] We are going to learn our lesson today by stacking together unusual pictures and words, and then using them in a short story. It's called Stack, Link, and Laugh. You will be amazed at your increased capacity to remember information by using this technique. Voilà! Right before your eyes, you'll see a genius emerging—and it will be *you*! You see, the best way to remember information is to link it to an image so ridiculous and fun that the brain can't possibly forget the facts! And that is precisely what we are going to do.

How will we do this? Let's say, for example, that we want to remember the names of the five oceans. Sure, we could memorize them, but how long do you think you'd remember them? Probably just long enough to answer the test questions. Here's another way to do it. [Write the following story on the board.]

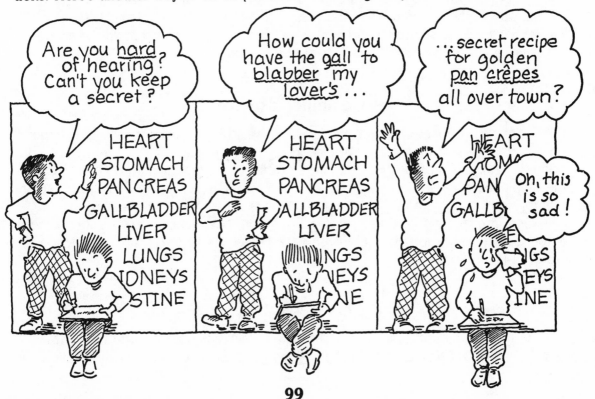

The Five Oceans

Once upon a time, there was a man named <u>Art-tic</u> (Arctic) who developed a tic due to his occupation of pole sitting. His tic was a real nuisance to his wife, whom everyone affectionately called <u>Aunt Art-tic</u> (Antarctic). Whenever Art-tic would talk, his tic would cause him to mumble. Aunt Art-tic would heave a big sigh and say, "Can you be more <u>specific</u>?" (Pacific). She finally couldn't stand it any longer. She decided to go on a long trip as far away from poor Art-tic as possible, <u>and landed</u> (Atlantic) on a totem pole, where she now lives with <u>Indians</u> (Indian).

Now, do you see how easy and painless that was to learn? Let's all read it together. How many of you now know all five oceans? Great! You'll probably never forget them either! Now let's apply this idea to the [rules, terms, concepts, words— depending on the subject matter] that we have been learning.

[We have included three more examples to help get you started.]

Seven Gases in the Air

Late one <u>night, a Trojan</u> (nitrogen) slept near his dependable <u>ox again</u> (oxygen), outside the city of Troy. The warrior woke up, looked for his weapons, and said, "They <u>are gone</u>!" (argon). He was so angry that he burned his food. He carried his <u>charred buns</u> on his <u>ox hide</u> (carbon dioxide). He had to follow his fellow soldiers. On his way to the wooden horse, he met a friend and said, "<u>Hi, Trojan</u>!" (hydrogen). As they walked, he stumbled and cut his <u>knee on</u> (neon) a sharp rock. His friend gave him a potion, hoping it would <u>heal him</u> (helium).

A Computer Experience

The trendy, upbeat computer family of <u>Disk</u> and <u>Diskette</u> went for a short spin on an impulse—sort of a <u>disk drive</u>, according to <u>Micro-chip</u>, their little one with big potential. A quick stop at the hardware store let Disk <u>monitor</u> the process of <u>CPU</u>, the employee who was in control of the business. While checking things out, the <u>Memory</u> sisters, <u>RAM</u> and <u>ROM</u>, came in to recall their Vegas trip and report the <u>slots</u> and <u>interface cards</u>. One swift <u>hardboot</u> from Micro-chip, and CPU lost a tooth. Now his <u>byte</u> will be off—he will have to take little <u>bits</u> and skip the <u>math</u> action —oh no! He lispths!

A Nerve Cell

The <u>Newron</u> (neuron) family was planning a reunion. Art Newron didn't know how he would get to the party at <u>Spinal Junction</u> (spinal cord) as his car needed a new <u>motor</u> (motor neuron). Luckily, Bob Newron had the <u>sense</u> (sensory neuron) to invite him to travel with him to the party. They had a good <u>association</u> (association neuron). On the way, they had an accident because Bob's <u>reflexes</u> (reflex) weren't good. They put <u>dents right</u> (dendrites) in the car, and the door had to be <u>axed</u> (axon) open. The police put them into a <u>cell</u> with the warning that it was a <u>sin</u> (synapse) to speed.

Variations

Have students create a Stack, Link, and Laugh story as a group. You can use twenty-five words or concepts per story. Or divide the class into groups of six. Each group takes five to eight concepts and creates a Stack, Link, and Laugh story and then teaches it to the rest of the class.

5. Dr. Genius

Overview

The word *genius* is an intriguing and often misunderstood word. Some people associate genius with an innate quality belonging only to a privileged few. And, yet, brain research is replete with evidence that we all have hidden genius, and that we use less than 5 percent of our mental capacity. This activity will bring out the hidden genius in everyone and add a tremendous richness to any lesson.

Activity

[Say to students:] How many of you believe that you have hidden genius within you? [Usually this question evokes laughter, although the very young will raise their hands unabashedly!] I believe that there are tremendous reservoirs of ideas of genius waiting to be uncovered within each of you. We're going to play a game that will help bring out your genius. It's called Dr. Genius. I'd like you to imagine that you are a world-renowned genius, and that you have made a discovery or have invented something new. The world is eating out of your hand and rolling out the red carpet everywhere you go.

I'll give you a few moments to think about what you have discovered. Maybe it's a cure for AIDS or an amazing new physics discovery, or perhaps you have created a telecommunication tool that can decipher extraterrestrial languages. Your invention can be as practical or as crazy as you would like it to be. Once you know your discovery or invention, we will call you Doctor [student chooses a name].

[Props of some sort are very useful, such as white shirts with students' Doctor names written on the back, hats made out of construction paper with the names written on the front, or name tags.]

[Have all the students choose a name and a "discovery," and then give them the following instructions.]

When we play Dr. Genius, answer all questions and participate in class as your genius character. Ask questions about topics that would interest your character, and call your classmates by their Dr. Genius titles as well. Think, move, and breathe the way your character would. I will also be portraying a character, though we all know, as your loyal and humble teacher, I am already a genius! You will be amazed at your ideas and thoughts as Dr. Genius. In your other classes, you may be considered an average student, but don't ever utter that obscenity in this room. When you walk into this classroom, in character, you become a genius. Albert Einstein, watch out!

Variations

Have your students pick a new Dr. Genius character each month. Or have students write some of their homework assignments as their character, especially if it is an assignment that allows for commentary. This adds a dimension of humor, insight, and intelligence that will take your students way beyond their "ordinary capacities."

6. Mind Mapping

Overview

Research has shown that the brain remembers patterns more easily than linear images, such as rows of words or paragraphs. We believe that in the future, this Laughing Lesson will be a mandatory skill for all learners. The genius of Mind Mapping is that it combines, in a stimulating way, both visual images and information.

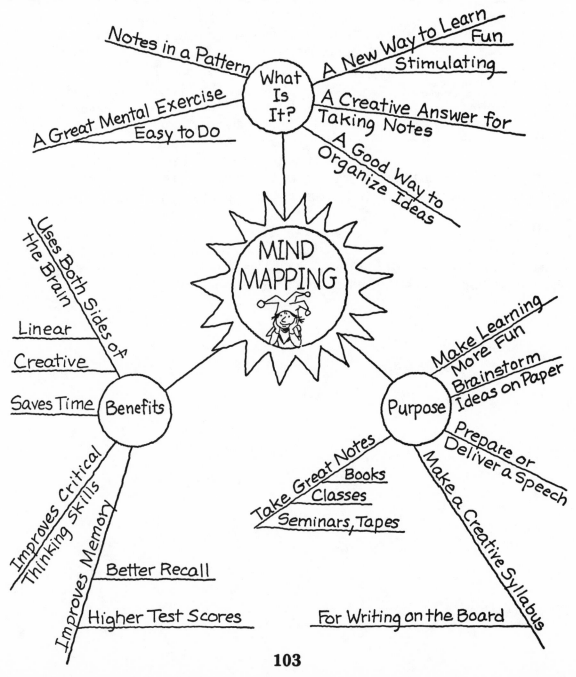

Activity

[Say to students:] Please notice that on the board I have written today's lesson in a pattern, rather than in lines. This is called Mind Mapping. It is a very creative and useful way to take notes and remember information. You'll see that I have handed out white paper [approximately 9"×12"] so that you can try Mind Mapping for yourselves. [Use information from a chapter, an outline, a few pages of text, or whatever is appropriate.] Please feel free to create any shape that you would like—circles, squares, or even simple designs such as trees, mountains, or clouds. The idea is to integrate your subject matter into the design or the shapes. For an added memory boost, color in your Mind Mapping after you finish mapping the information. You will be amazed at your ability to remember this information. Are there any questions? Okay, let's get started.

Humor is emotional chaos remembered in tranquility.
– James Thurber

[You may want to hand students photocopies from a simple coloring book drawing to get your class started. As they progress, they will become very innovative about creating designs for themselves.]

Variations

Hand out the syllabus or review sheets Mind Mapping style, or create a group Mind Mapping on the board to review for a test. After students get the hang of it, have them turn in an assignment using a Mind Mapping style.

7. Creative Debate

Overview

A good debate is a great way to stimulate the mind and to get the blood flowing! This Laughing Lesson will bring a whole new world of ideas and perspectives into the classroom. It is especially suited to courses that require more than one perspective, such as history, science, psychology, or communications classes.

Activity

[Say to students:] Today we are going to approach our class discussion in a unique way. Will the first two rows [how you gather ten to twelve students is up to you] please bring your chairs up to the front of the room so that row one faces row two. Does everybody understand me so far? Great! Now, our issue in debate today is going to be [choose a relevant topic].

Row one, you will be "for" the issue, and row two, you will be "against" it. But this will not just be an ordinary debate. I am going to ask you to decide upon a character from the past, present, or future who supports the position that you are taking—either for or against. In our debate, you will become this character for the sake of a lively discussion. It's okay if you do not agree with the side that you are given. All the better, because it will help you to see from a different perspective. If you like, you can take on the posture, voice, or mannerisms of your character, but the most important thing is that you represent that character's perspective on the issue under discussion.

I'll give you a few minutes to decide upon a character while we think about questions to ask you. You will respond to any questions asked only if "the spirit moves you." After about ten minutes of discussion between rows one and two, the rest of the class can ask a question of either row, or of a particular character. Before we begin the debate, I'd like you to introduce yourself, as your character, to the rest of the class.

Variations

Have the class split into teams and carry on smaller debates without an audience. Or plan the event ahead of time so that the debate teams can come dressed in appropriate costumes, having researched phrases and gestures for their characters.

8. The Wizard

Overview

Any teaching unit can be enhanced by using this lighthearted Laughing Lesson. The Wizard is a wonderful alternative to the usual stand-up oral report. The students must listen closely to one another and work as a team to answer questions successfully. Even if their answers aren't always logical or accurate, the laughter evoked by the often funny responses helps to disperse any tension created by giving a report in front of a group.

Activity

[Say to students:] We have been studying [the example here is famous African-American leaders] in this month's unit, and each brainstorming group has researched a famous leader. As a part of your oral presentation, you will have the opportunity to answer several questions as the Wizard.

Will the first group of four come up to the front of the room and stand next to one another, shoulder to shoulder. You are now transformed into the Wizard! Although you have four bodies, you have only one mind. We are going to ask you several questions, and, as the Wizard, you will answer as best you can. You are allowed to speak only *one word at a time*. The person standing at the end of the Wizard's line will begin. You must listen closely to one another and add your word to the sentence, so that the sentence makes sense. Remember, you are trying to answer the question as well as you possibly can. Example:

Question: Who was Dr. Martin Luther King, Jr.?

Wizard's Answer:

Student #1 He	Student #2 was	Student #3 a	Student #4 famous
Student #1 black	Student #2 leader	Student #3 who	Student #4 said,
Student #1 "I	Student #2 have	Student #3 a	Student #4 dream."

Variations

This exercise can be played with two people transforming into the Wizard. The students speak one word at a time, until they have explained their information or given their report. It's even more interesting to have two Wizards (two groups of two) conversing with each other. One Wizard can be the New Wizard and ask the other Wizard questions. Remember, you do not have to spend a tremendous amount of time playing a game to receive its beneficial effects. Just opening a presentation with this technique will be enough. Make sure that you always set a time limit on the games; otherwise, everyone will want to play them for hours.

9. "Functuation"

Overview

As a part of his comedy routine, Victor Borge reads a passage from a story and uses his voice to create sounds for the punctuation. Audiences love this brilliant routine so much that they insist he perform it before he leaves the stage. We've adapted his method to help make learning punctuation more fun.

Activity

[Say to students:] How many of you have ever made strange sounds with your mouths or voices? Today, we are going to put your vocal talents to use. We are going to create sounds or sound effects for all the different types of punctuation. Who can create a sound for a comma? Let's all try to imitate that sound. What about a period? A question mark? A colon and semicolon? How about dashes and dots? Great. Let's not forget the exclamation point!

I'm handing you a sheet with twenty sentences that have no punctuation marks. I'd like you to take the next few minutes to put the punctuation marks where you think they belong. Then you'll get a chance to read a sentence of your choice aloud. But instead of telling me where the marks should go, you will vocally place the marks where you think they should be. This way, instead of seeing it, we'll hear it. Let's review the sounds one more time before we begin.

Variations

Instead of using vocal sound effects, which may be difficult for some students, gather a series of noise-makers, such as a horn, a bell, a duck call, a slide whistle, and so forth. Give each kind of punctuation a sound effect, and then let the students punctuate passages. You can have one student in charge of the sound effects or give sound makers to several students. If the person with the horn is responsible for commas, then anytime he or she feels there should be a comma in a sentence, that student plays the horn.

Did the ship *bwitt* full of angry pirates *zwoop* including Captain Punk *zwoop bwitt* sail into the sunset *tluck*

10. Student Scholar

Overview

If you've ever watched television talk shows, you've probably noticed that human beings love to express their thoughts, share their feelings, and talk about what they know or "think" they know. This Laughing Lesson plays into this human desire with some very funny results. The goal of the game is to motivate students to learn enough about a given topic so that they can pretend to be an expert or scholar.

This technique can be used in several ways. You can use it purely as an entertainment piece to promote laughter or energize the group, or you can use it as a teaching tool to enhance your core curriculum. If you use it the first way, the two Student Scholars speak to the class as if they know everything about a chosen topic (although they know very little). Or you can require students to research a topic thoroughly. Only after they have proven to you that they understand the information are they allowed to become Student Scholars.

Activity

[This exercise requires two students. One student is the vocal Student Scholar and answers the questions from the class. The other student crouches behind the speaker and becomes the scholar's hands. This is done by having the "hands" person stand behind the scholar, bending the knees slightly so the head doesn't show. The scholar raises his or her arms, and the "hands" person slips his or her arms underneath and through the scholar's arms (as if replacing the scholar's own arms and hands). The scholar then wraps his or her arms around the person behind him or her. The two students have now become one. To complete the illusion, you can throw a coat, sweater, or cloth over the head of the person acting as the scholar's hands. This assures that only the Student Scholar's head will be seen. The hands can guide and follow the Student Scholar, but it should look as if the hands were the scholar's hands.]

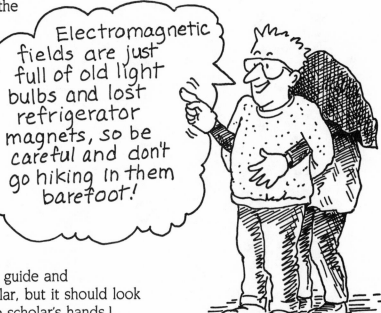

Electromagnetic fields are just full of old light bulbs and lost refrigerator magnets, so be careful and don't go hiking in them barefoot!

[Say to students:] Today, we have the privilege of speaking with the Student Scholar. He/she will be discussing [example: electromagnetic fields]. I'd like you to write one question that you have about his/her field of expertise, and the Student Scholar will answer your questions to the best of his/her knowledge. Please pass the questions up to the front for the Student Scholar. Student Scholar, you can pick five questions to answer.

Variations

Assign historical figures, literary personalities, contemporary politicians, artists, or pop idols to sets of Student Scholars. Give them a topic of discussion, and have two sets of scholars converse or debate.

A good laugh is
sunshine in a house.
– Thackeray

11. Moving Minds

Overview

This Laughing Lesson combines storytelling, visualization, humor, and movement to help students encode and retain information. When you use the five senses to stimulate the brain, the information is encoded in different lobes. The wider the range of encoding, the easier it is to recall information. For maximum retention, the story/information should be presented in chunks and repeated at least once a week for several weeks. As a pleasant benefit, dances are often created spontaneously from the movements that emerge during class.

Don't reveal to the students what they are learning until after the exercise. Most of the time they will guess, but it's fun if they don't know until after they have learned the movements. After they have memorized the story and the movements, you can have them do just the movements without the story. The students will easily be able to remember the sequence, whether you start from the beginning, middle, or end of the story.

Activity

[The following example uses the nine planets.]
[Say to students:] I'm going to tell you a story today, and I'd like you to use your imaginations to see what I'm describing. We are also going to create movements to add to the story. We'll practice these movements several times. Every time you hear the word that has a movement created for it, you do the movement. Are you ready?

I'd like you to imagine a very *Murky* river. It's so *Murky* that you can't see the bottom of it. You definitely wouldn't want to swim in this *Murky* water. What kind of hand or body movement

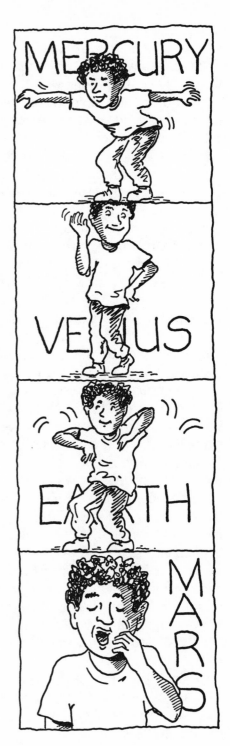

can we create for the *Murky* river? [Have a movement in mind in case the students don't have any ideas. Have them repeat the movement several times and repeat the words *Murky* river along with the movement.]

Standing knee deep in the *Murky* river is a statue of *Venus*. [For a guaranteed laugh, try a Mae West movement; place your hand on one hip and fluff your hair with the other.] Now *Venus* [do movement] is very gorgeous, but she's standing in this awful, polluted, *Murky* [movement] water. *Venus* [movement] is unaware that the river is rising. *Venus* [movement] is too busy fluffing her hair.

Besides, *Venus* [movement], who is standing in this *Murky* [movement] water, lacks eyes. She only has eye sockets. And crawling in and out of her eye sockets are *Earthworms* [create a movement for *Earthworms*]. Where are the *Earthworms* [movement] crawling? That's right. Inside the eye sockets of *Venus* [movement], who is standing in the *Murky* [movement] water.

These creepy, crawly *Earthworms* [movement] live on candy bars. If you look really closely into the eye sockets of *Venus* [movement], you'll notice the *Earthworms* [movement] are eating *Mars* bars. (Let's create a movement for how *Earthworms* [movement] would eat *Mars* [movement] bars. Good.) So, the *Mars* [movement] bars are being eaten by the *Earthworms* [movement], inside *Venus* [movement], who is standing knee-deep in *Murky* [movement] water.

Precariously balanced on top of *Venus'* [movement] head is a bright red *Jewel*. (Let's make a hand movement to show the *Jewel*.) This *Jewel* [movement] is so bright you have to shield your eyes when you look at it. Suddenly, the *Jewel* [movement] starts to spin. And as it spins, the *Mars* [movement] bars are flung out of the mouths of the *Earthworms* [movement], who are in the eyes of *Venus* [movement], who is in the *Murky* [movement] water.

When the *Jewel* [movement] finally stops spinning, you see that attached to it is a flashing yellow neon sign that says "*Saturday, Saturday, Saturday.*" (Let's create another movement for the flashing *Saturday* sign.) What's flashing? The yellow neon *Saturday* [movement] sign.

Then it begins to *Rain and Rain and Rain*. (How can we show *Rain*?) It's not ordinary *Rain* [movement]. It's purple *Rain* [movement]. It starts *Raining* so hard, you can no longer see the flashing *Saturday* [movement] sign that's attached to the red *Jewel* [movement] or the *Mars* [movement] bars inside the mouths of the *Earthworms* [movement]. All you see is *Venus* [movement], who now notices that the *Murky* [movement] water is rising.

From the depths of the *Murky* [movement] water comes *Neptune*. (Let's come up with a movement for *Neptune*. He's quite large and carries a three-pronged spear.) He's there to stop the purple *Rain* [movement] from hiding the flashing *Saturday* [movement] sign on the red *Jewel* [movement], and so the *Mars* [movement] bars won't be washed right out of the mouths of the *Earthworms* [movement]. He came to save *Venus* [movement] from drowning in the *Murky* [movement] water.

In his hand is a tiny Walt Disney character named *Pluto*. (How can we show *Pluto*?)

112

Pluto [movement] waves at *Venus* [movement] and then barks the tiniest bark. You can hardly hear *Pluto's* [movement] bark. When *Pluto* [movement], who is resting in the hand of *Neptune* [movement], barks, the *Rain* [movement] stops. The clouds disperse, and you can again see the flashing yellow *Saturday* [movement] sign on the red *Jewel* [movement], which begins to spin again. The *Mars* [movement] bars are no longer melting, so the *Earthworms* [movement] bring out another case to eat inside the eyes of *Venus* [movement], who is now smiling because the *Murky* [movement] water was just about at her chin and threatened to carry her downstream.

Variations

You can use this technique to present complex information that needs to be memorized, including anatomical facts about skeletal and vascular systems, legal terms, the states and their capitals, or the periodic table. A classroom of thirty-five third graders learned the names of the presidents using this method. They became so excited about what they had learned that the fourth, fifth, and sixth grades insisted that they be taught the "Presidents' Dance."

12. Manikin

Overview

Children increase their capacity to concentrate when they perform activities that are fun, creative, and challenging. The one requirement for this Laughing Lesson is that the person playing the Manikin must stand perfectly still for a short period. You'll be surprised how this game can calm down even the most hyperactive child. Even the most aloof teenagers will stand still and allow others to manipulate them if it's done in the spirit of play. It's a safe way for a student to receive attention by simply standing still. This "live" Manikin method can be used as a springboard for discussions about the subject matter you are presently covering.

Activity

[Say to students:] Which of you thinks that you can stand perfectly still for more than two minutes? Well, come on up, and we'll give you a chance. Everyone here has seen a department-store manikin, right? On the count of three, [person's name] will magically transform into a Manikin. Notice, I did not say department-store *dummy*. Ready? One, two, three. Good. Now, if I say to [person's name], "Please raise your right arm," he/she will not respond. Even if I stand in front of him/her and try to make him/her laugh—no response. By the way, Manikin, you can blink, swallow, and, please, keep breathing! Now, the great thing about this Manikin is that I can manipulate him/her. If I move his/her arm up over his/her head, it stays there. See? If I lower it, it also stays there. I can make the Manikin bend, twist, smile, frown, or look as if he/she thinks the sky is falling. Very good, Manikin. I can even pick the Manikin up and move it to a different spot. [Do this only with small children.]

We've been studying [example: what happens to the body when it's under stress]. Who wants to come up and place the Manikin in a position that would show us how a person would look if he or she were experiencing stress? [A student manipulates the Manikin into a new position.] Thanks, Manikin. You did a great job. Shake out any sore muscles. [You may want to have a few students move the Manikin into different positions.]

Variations

You can create a human "still life," also known as a tableau, with many Manikins. (Five or six is the optimal number for a tableau.) This is usually done as an add-on process, when you or your students place one Manikin into a position and place the other Manikin in relation to it. Once you have the still life or "frozen photograph" set, you can use the image to create short stories or poems, or use it to talk about family dynamics or conflict resolution. You can give the manipulators of the Manikins a concept to work with, or they can create something new. If the Manikins can stay focused, you can ask them to answer a few questions, such as: Who are you in this scene? What's happening here? What are you thinking? What happened right before you were frozen? Then you tap a Manikin on the shoulder, and that one steps out and tells his or her version of the story. You can have all the Manikins in the tableau relate the ideas that came to them as they stood there, or you can select a central character in the scene. The possibilities for this Laughing Lesson are as endless as your imagination!

Laugh with a vast and inextinguishable laughter. — Shelley

13. Tag-Team Talk

Overview

If you've seen a tag-team All Star Wrestling match, then you have a good idea of how to play this Laughing Lesson. When a player on one team runs out of steam, he or she tags a teammate, and the teammate jumps into the center ring to take over where the other left off. This is a very fast exercise and can be used for reviewing facts or for presenting two sides of an argument.

Activity

[Say to students:] Today we are going to debate [example: an individual's right to bear arms]. I'm going to divide the class in half. The right half is "against" [bearing arms], and the left half is "for" [bearing arms]. Even if you do not agree with the position you've been given, you still have to argue your position effectively. We are going to use Tag-Team Talk to get as many arguments for and against the issue out on the table as quickly as possible. So be ready to hop up and help your teammates if they run out of steam.

Here is the way it works. I need one person from each side of the debate to stand in front of the room. Please face each other but stand an arm and a half's length away. The "pro" side is going to argue a point, and the "con" side has to counter it with another point. Bring to the floor as many different arguments as you can. When you run out of ideas or feel as if you can't find the right words to counter an argument effectively, you simply hold out your hand, palm up. This is the signal for any one of your teammates to "tag in" and take over the argument for

116

you. You can "tag out" immediately if you're stumped, or you can stay in the debate as long as you like. If one of your teammates wants to tag in, he or she will approach the front and hold out a hand, palm up, signaling to you to step out of the center ring while he or she takes over. You now have five minutes to debate.

Variations

You can divide your class into two large teams and allow anyone who has an idea, an argument, or a fact to jump in. Or you can play a simplified version with only four members per team and the rest of the class as observers. The numbers you choose for teams will depend upon the lesson you are teaching and the type of material you want to cover.

14. Gibberish Interpreter

Overview

This is another experts' Laughing Lesson. If, as a child, you pretended to speak a foreign language that you didn't know, you were speaking "Gibberish." Adults often speak Gibberish to infants. It's a playful way to communicate without words, because this nonsense language is composed of words that sound authentic but that the speaker has invented. Try to say this sentence aloud: "*Asticfon nis olan comotooto aranto parta nolo.*" Try saying the sentence with various accents—French, Italian, German, Russian, or Swedish. You have just spoken Gibberish! It's fun to speak Gibberish because there is no right or wrong way to speak it. The person speaking Gibberish is free to create, because the responsibility for accurately relaying the information always falls upon the translator. So be sure to allow everyone to try both parts.

Activity

[You'll need two students to play Gibberish Interpreter. One student speaks Gibberish, and the other translates the Gibberish into English. Before playing the game, it's best to practice speaking Gibberish so that everyone feels comfortable with the form. You can practice by using the call-and-response method. You, or your students, create Gibberish sentences that everyone repeats. Remember, exaggeration is more important than accuracy. It will only take a few minutes before everyone understands the game.]

[Say to students:] We have just finished studying [example: the world's deserts]. Today, you're going to review what we've covered, but you are going to get a chance to review the information using Gibberish Interpreter. Who would like to answer questions about what we've learned?

I'll need two volunteers. Great. Student Number One, you are going to speak Gibberish, and Student Number Two, you are going to translate what your partner has just said. Remember, your partner doesn't speak a word of English, so he or she won't understand the questions you ask. [Example: Which desert do you want to talk about today?] The Sahara Desert? Fine. First, you need to call on someone who has a question about the Sahara. Next, you'll have to translate the question into your partner's language. Your partner will then answer using Gibberish and mime. It's your job to tell us what your partner said and to answer the question.

Let me start by introducing the two of you to your classmates. Good afternoon, everyone. Today we are lucky to have as our guests Ms. [insert name] from the Sahara Desert. She would love to answer any questions you have about the desert, but unfortunately she doesn't speak English. Mr. [insert name] will be her translator. Do any of you have a question about the Sahara that you would like answered?

Variations

Instead of two students, you could set up a panel of experts who speak Gibberish. One or more students could translate for the panel. It's also fun for two students to converse in Gibberish, with a translator in the middle interpreting for both parties. Two students (one as translator) could speak to another student who is speaking through a translator. As a lesson in government, you could create an environment such as the United Nations and debate important issues using translators.

15. Brainstorming Buddies

Overview

Peer group counseling has proved to be a positive way for kids to help each other. Why not start a positive mentoring system so that children can support and assist one another? The purpose of this Laughing Lesson is to show students that no one has all the answers to all the questions all the time. If done in a playful way, it can be a wonderful brain boost to those who don't believe in their abilities. It gives students a chance to see what's "right" with themselves and the world instead of focusing on what's "wrong," or what's not working. The most challenging part of this Laughing Lesson is finding a fun and creative way to pair students so that everyone feels important. It's helpful if the buddies like each other, but it won't be as effective if they are "best friends."

Activity

[Say to students:] You are now sitting next to the most incredible human being on the face of this planet (other than you, of course). That person is your Brainstorming Buddy. Your Buddy is in charge of the care and feeding of your brain. What does this mean? At any time during class, starting now until the end of the year, I will sometimes call out, "Brainstorming Buddies!" When I do this, you'll have ten seconds to get together with your Buddy, create a secret handshake or greeting, and then wait for instructions.

Before I give you an assignment, I'd like to share some thoughts about your Brainstorming Buddy. Your Buddy is always supportive. No matter how negative you may feel about yourself or your life, your Buddy believes in you and supports your growth one hundred percent. Your Buddy always has one or two great ideas that will help you be more successful. Your Buddy believes in confidentiality. Nothing you tell your Buddy will ever leave this room. Your Buddy will try to help you if you ever have a problem, but, most important, your Buddy truly likes you as you are now and likes who you are becoming.

[Example: On the board are ten new vocabulary words that need defining.] I'd like you and your Buddy to take the next ten minutes to do the following: Write the real

120

definition for each word and then create ridiculous and outrageous definitions for those ten words. You have ten minutes. Don't forget to compliment your Buddy for being so brilliant. After all, you are now certified Brainstorming Buddies.

Variations

> It is bad to suppress laughter. It goes back down and spreads to your hips. – Steve Allen

Form Brainstorming Groups instead of Buddies. Give these groups a chance to meet once a week to share their success stories and to encourage one another. Ask them to create a playful or funny name for their groups, such as "The Big Brains" or "Dig Dem Dendrites." They can also create a hand signal, a sound effect, a favorite saying, or anything else that helps them feel more like a brain support group. They might also want to create an imaginary "Board of Brains." They could have Albert Einstein, Mark Twain, Mahatma Gandhi, or other notables as a part of their mentor circle.

25

Play Breaks

Brain research has shown that learning occurs with greater ease if it is segmented into fifteen-minute to forty-five-minute units and followed by three- to five-minute breaks. This gives the brain a chance to sort and integrate the new material. Play Breaks provide a fun "brain breather." Students of all ages will look forward to these few playful minutes the way they look forward to their recess or lunch break!

Play Breaks play two major functions. They increase energy levels that may be at a low ebb because of physical inactivity, and they help reduce stress and anxiety responses caused by fear.

Although low-level stress can increase alertness, high-level stress can cause deterioration or disorganization. This response sometimes occurs with athletes who "choke" or lose control at strategic moments because of their heightened anxiety. It's important to recognize that the learning process can be threatening for students. Tests and the pressure to perform often cause stress. High anxiety alienates the slow learner and frustrates the fast one.

To facilitate learning, a balance between lethargy and anxiety must be maintained. A state of "heightened preparedness" can be obtained by inserting Play Breaks into your teaching day. They will energize the group, increase retention, make learning more enjoyable, and improve student morale. This chapter contains tried-and-true ideas for you to use with your classes. Please note that many Play Breaks and Warm-ups can be used interchangeably.

1. Tongue Twisters

Overview

Lawrence Olivier used to recite Tongue Twisters before he went on stage to help him overcome his terrible stage fright. He claimed that doing this helped him to relax and become more "mentally fluent." Reciting Tongue Twisters seems to have the same effect on students. Try a few the next time your students need a change of pace and a few laughs!

Activity

[Say to students:] We're going to recite several Tongue Twisters to synchronize our brains with our tongues. You'll notice there are three Tongue Twisters written on the board. [See the Tongue Twisters List for Tongue Twisters you might use.] Find a partner, preferably someone who hasn't played this game with you before. Okay, does everyone have a partner? Good. Now, whoever has larger feet [anything can be substituted] will be Partner Number One. You will recite the first Tongue Twister, three times in a row, as quickly as you can. Are you ready? We'll take ten seconds. Start right now. Okay, now it's time to give your partner a chance to recite the second Tongue Twister, three times in a row, as quickly as possible. Get ready, partners; get set; go! Now, for the last Tongue Twister. Both of you will recite the third Tongue Twister aloud as quickly as you can. Start right now!

Tongue Twisters List:
Trip Thy Tongue Through These Titillating Twisters.

Double bubble gum bubbles double.
You know New York. You need New York. You know you need unique New York.
Sixty-six sick chicks.
Strange strategic statistic.
Tie twine to three tree twigs.
Preshrunk shirts.
Shy Sarah saw six Swiss wristwatches.
The sixth sheikh's sixth sheep's sick.
Truly rural.
The seething sea ceaseth, and thus seething
   sea sufficeth us.
A bloke's back brake block broke.
Does this shop stock short socks with spots?
Three gray geese in the green grass grazing;
   gray were the geese, and green was the grazing.
Sinful Caesar sipped his snifter, seized his knees,
   and sneezed.

Fanny Fowler tried five floundering fish for Francis Finch's father.

A big black bug bit a big black bear—made a big black bear bleed blood.

A skunk stood on a stump. The stump thunk the skunk stunk, but the skunk thunk the stump stunk.

Variations

Have students create their own Tongue Twisters based on the material that they are learning in school.

Or have them create a Tongue Twister using the names of classmates, such as, "Billy boy bottles blue bacon on the bayou." This Tongue Twister was created by a fifth-grade class. For fun, time students to see who can recite them the fastest.

2. Sixty-Second "Mirth-Quake"

Overview

Sometimes, on rainy, low-energy days, a good old-fashioned belly laugh is what's needed. The Sixty-Second "Mirth-Quake" is a great way to teach students the value of taking a few minutes to lighten up before learning. It can be an invigorating, habit-forming experience!

Activity

[Say to students:] Let's stand for a moment and stretch a little. That's right, put your whole body into it. To stretch our mental muscles, we're going to create a "Mirth-Quake." Oliver Wendell Holmes said, "The mind, once stretched to a new proportion, never returns to its original dimension." So let's start out in silence with a small smile—just the hint of a grin—not too much now. This will crack the mental ice. Now, without making a sound, turn to someone and smile. Go ahead. I dare you to smile at someone without a peep! Good. Next, let's silently move as if we're laughing. That's right. Aren't you beginning to feel better already?

And now, let's move into a state of silent hilariousness. Act as if you're caught in a fit of laughter. Exaggerate your body movements; tilt your head back, slap your knee—you know, go the whole nine yards. That's it. Now we're starting to shake the laughter loose. Finally, add sound to your motions, and let out a long, loud, luxurious laugh! You can fake it until you make it, if you'd like! Go ahead. Let it out. Great! Don't you feel better? Now we're ready to go back to learning, with our lungs expanded and our minds stretched. We need to do this much more often.

Variations

Have students pair off, face each other, and mime the "Mirth-Quake" motions. Or have students pair off, and have one person laugh silently while the other watches stone faced. This always brings laughter and seems to remind us of the times we couldn't stop laughing despite our good intentions to remain silent.

Laughter shows us that we are more important than our problems.
– José Ferrer

3. Classroom Storyteller

Overview

Everyone loves to hear a good story. In the past, information was often passed along through storytelling; this remains an integral part of many cultures throughout the world. Here is a great way to bring this lost art regularly into the classroom. All ages, from two to ninety-two, will enjoy this activity.

Activity

[Say to students:] We're going to take a storytelling break. I've written several sample categories on the board. Please choose a category for today.

Sample Categories

1. Incredible coincidences
2. Scientific wonders
3. Personal stories
4. Hilarious and true
5. Embarrassing episodes
6. Clean joke of the day
7. Strange and true

Do any of you have a story that you would like to share from one of these categories? Remember to limit the story to three minutes or less. If someone has a very short joke or story, perhaps we'll have time for a few. [If no one volunteers, have a story prepared. Once your group gets the hang of this, you'll never get a chance to get a word in edgewise. There are usually students waiting to tell stories once you teach them this game.]

Variations

Let students create new categories to add variety to the game. Or pick a category and have pairs of students tell each other a story.

4. Conducting

Overview

This is a high-energy Play Break for groups with members who are familiar with one another and feel comfortable working and laughing together. Select a two- to three-minute piece of lively, up-tempo music without lyrics. We recommend that you choose a classical piece or one that starts out slowly, but increases in tempo [example· "The Hall of the Mountain King"].

Activity

[Say to students:] We're going to take a musical Play Break that will make us feel like dancing throughout the day. Are you ready? Please stand up and stretch. Great! Let's stretch all our muscles as we prepare to listen to the following piece of music. We're going to be listening in a unique way. We're going to imagine that we are listening to the music as if we were the conductor.

[Begin playing the music.] Imagine the intense feeling that courses through the veins of conductors as they listen to the instruments and work to blend them into an auditory masterpiece! Imagine that you have arranged the piece of music that you're now hearing. You may listen to the music with your eyes closed if you like. As the music plays, feel yourself coming to life. Listen with a new intensity and skill. Begin to move your hands with the music as though you were conducting an orchestra. That's right. Start to move

your elbows and arms. Let yourself feel the music flowing through you as you conduct. Move your whole body, allowing yourself to respond, spontaneously, to the sounds you are hearing. Feel proud of your fine accomplishment.

And now, as the music ends, open your eyes and give yourself an ovation for outstanding conducting.

Variations

If you want to add another dimension to this exercise, have the students use unsharpened pencils or rulers as conducting wands. Or, for a wildly outrageous experience, pass around a two-ply roll of toilet paper about ten minutes before the conducting Play Break. Ask the students to tear off strips the length of their arms. Have them pull their strips apart so that they have two strips, one for each hand. As the music starts, they conduct using their toilet paper wands. This creates a very humorous visual effect. This idea will brighten even a classroom filled with sleepwalkers.

5. Crazy Questions

Overview

Crazy Questions help to develop two important elements of the creative process—fluency and flexibility. Fluency is the ability to generate ideas freely, while flexibility is the ability to see from a variety of perspectives. Brain research studies show that the brain often responds more readily to a question than to an answer. This exercise encourages fluent, flexible thinking while stimulating the brain.

Activity

[Say to students:] Let's open our minds, relax our bodies, and prepare to flex our creativity muscles. I'm going to ask you a Crazy Question, and I'd like you to give your answer to a partner. Will everyone please find a partner? Whoever has longer earlobes [anything can be substituted] will answer first. When you're finished, your partner will then answer the question. You have one minute to create an answer. Don't be afraid to say the first thing that comes to your mind. There are no right answers—only crazy answers to Crazy Questions. The first Crazy Question is . . .

Examples of Crazy Questions

1. What bumper sticker slogan would you like to see on the back of a tractor?
2. Which tree would you rather be? A palm tree, an oak tree, or a weeping willow?
3. Which is bolder—an "X," a "Y," or a "Z"? Why?
4. Would you rather be a flying fish or a running turtle? Why?
5. How are cold icy days and talking parrots alike?
6. If you could be any animal in the world for an hour, which would you be? Why?
7. What does an ant want most to say to the elephant next to it?
8. When is backward really forward?
9. Which is quieter—the clear blue sky, the color violet, or the sound of one hand clapping?
10. Which color tastes better—red or green? Why?
11. If you could step into any movie for one hour and make it come to life, which movie would you pick? Why?
12. If you could be a door, a window, or a hole in the ceiling, which would you be? Why?

Okay, now that you have all had a chance to answer the question with your partner, let's gather together and take a minute or two to share some of our crazy answers.

Variations

Make a Crazy Question box so that students can create questions for the game. Or, once students know how the game is played, ask for a volunteer to spontaneously create a Crazy Question.

6. Quote Quota

Overview

A good quotation is a compact, easily remembered bit of wisdom or inspiration. This activity will enrich the minds and hearts of participants and provide a minilesson in cultural and philosophical literacy. You might want to start this activity with a book of famous quotations. Soon, students will find quotations for Quote Quota from posters, slogans, advertisements, and, yes, even the classics.

Activity

[Say to students:] Let's stimulate our minds by sharing a few famous and a few obscure quotations. [Examples: Did you know that Abraham Lincoln once said, "If I had six hours to chop down a tree, I'd spend the first four hours sharpening the ax"? Or that Henry Ford once said, "If I lost everything, I'd start over and have it all back again in five years"?] Who has a quote to share with us? You can make up your own quote if you like. Here's one I created: "Heaven is putting yourself into the things you know you want to be doing. Hell is doing otherwise." [Give the group a few minutes to share quotes.] Does anyone remember who said this famous line from our last Quote Quota: "If you believe you can, you're right. If you believe you can't, you're right again!"

Variations

Have groups form two teams and alternately recite quotations and name their sources until a team runs out of quotes. Or, set up a playful question-and-answer period by creating two teams that must recite quotes from previous Quote Quota sessions. You award points to the team that correctly identifies the author of the quote. For inspiration, you can use the quotations that are included in this book.

"Never promise more than you can perform." MAXIM 528, PUBLILIUS SYRUS

7. Brain Benders

Overview

There's nothing like a Brain Bender for flexing brain biceps and stretching muscles that cause cerebral stiffness. Brain Benders get both sides of the brain involved, because the left side of the brain interprets the letters while the right side of the brain fills in the blanks with imagery. This is an excellent activity for a group that is suffering from Glove Compartment Brain Syndrome—useless "stuff" that often falls out of a brain when you open it.

Activity

[Say to students:] We're going to flex our brain biceps and solve a few Brain Benders. I've written five phrases on the blackboard. [See answers for your information in brackets.]

Sample Brain Benders

1. 26 L. of the A. [26 letters of the alphabet.]
2. 7 W. of the A. W. [7 wonders of the ancient world.]
3. 1,001 A. N. [1,001 Arabian Nights.]
4. 12 S. of the Z. [12 signs of the zodiac.]
5. 54 C. in a D. (with the Js.). [54 cards in a deck (with the jokers).]

Please look at the following sentences for the next three minutes. Do this silently. If you know the answers, please keep them to yourself so that everyone has a chance to guess them. Half the fun of these Brain Benders is experiencing the "Aha!" that happens when you find the answer. Just so you know how they work, I'll give the answer to the first one: twenty-six letters of the alphabet. Any other questions? Okay, let's get started.

[For your convenience, we have added nineteen more Brain Benders and answers for use in future Play Breaks.]

More Sample Brain Benders

1. 9 P. in the S. S. [9 planets in the solar system.]
2. 88 P. K. [88 piano keys.]
3. 13 S. on the A. F. [13 stripes on the American flag]
4. 32 D. F. at which W. F. [32 degrees Fahrenheit at which water freezes.]
5. 18 H. on a G. C. [18 holes on a golf course.]
6. 90 D. on a R. A. [90 degrees on a right angle.]
7. 200 D. for P. G. in M. [200 dollars for passing go in Monopoly.]

8. 8 S. on a S. S. [8 sides on a stop sign.]

9. 3 B. M. (S. H. T. R.). [3 blind mice (see how they run).]

10. 4 Q. in a G. [4 quarts in a gallon.]

11. 24 H. in a D. [24 hours in a day.]

12. 1 W. on a U. [1 wheel on a unicycle.]

13. 5 D. in a Z. C. [5 digits in a zip code.]

14. 57 H. V. [57 Heinz varieties.]

15. 11 P. on a F. T. [11 players on a football team.]

16. 1,000 W. is what a P. is W. [1,000 words is what a picture is worth.]

17. 29 D. in F. in a L. Y. [29 days in February in a leap year.]

18. 64 S. in a C. B. [64 squares in a checkerboard.]

19. 40 D. and N. of the G. F. [40 days and nights of the Great Flood.]

Variations

Have students create new Brain Benders and put them into a Brain Benders' box. When you have five or more, you can call a Brain Bender Play Break.

8. Pass the Drawing!

Overview

Drawing and doodling are fun activities that act as creative outlets and activate the imagination. This exercise requires students to collaborate; it results in the creation of three sketches from the "collective imagination" of your students. This Play Break is a hit with all ages from the young to the young at heart. You'll need enough paper and pencils or crayons for everyone.

Activity

[Say to students:] How many of you have ever drawn a picture with two other people? Well, you'll have a chance to do this during an activity called "Pass the Drawing." You must be in a group of three, so please find two other people, and then we'll begin. I'm going to give each of you a piece of paper. When I say, "Go," you'll have one minute to sketch whatever comes into your mind. If you like, it can be squares, circles, or squiggly shapes. Just start creating. Go! [Allow one minute.]

Stop! Now, I'd like you to pass your sheet to the right. You have exactly one minute to draw on this new sheet of paper. This new sheet should have something already drawn on it. Go! [Allow one minute.]

Stop! Now, pass your drawing to the right. The paper in front of you will have the work of two other artists on it. Again, you'll have one minute to add your unique sketching to this new drawing. Go! [Allow one minute.]

Stop! Now, pass the drawing to the right again, and you'll find that you have your original drawing. Observe how the additions of your co-artists have changed it. This is not an art contest, so it's best not to have any expectations about the finished piece. Take a close look at it. I'm going to give you one minute to explain to your group what you see in your new drawing. You'll really have to use your imagination, but that's the point. Enjoy it, whatever it is.

Variations

Lead the Pass the Drawing exercise as above, but allow the students to interpret their drawings based upon a theme, such as new inventions, wildest wishes, scariest dreams, or fondest memories.

Another variation is to have the students find part-ners and give each pair a large sheet of paper on which to work. Have them choose contrasting colored markers or crayons. The first person scribbles as fast as he or she can without picking the marker up from the paper. The goal of the second person is to follow or "chase" the lines closely while the first person draws. Then have the two reverse roles and have the second person scribble/run and the first person scribble/chase. The result will be peals of laughter.

The laughter of man is the contentment of God.   – John Weiss

9. What Are You Doing?

Overview

This Play Break is guaranteed to wake up and shake up your students. They will receive a mighty dose of cognitive dissonance, because their body is saying one thing while their brain is asserting the opposite. The result is a mental "implosion" and a physical "explosion" in the form of hearty laughter. It will take a few minutes of explanation to teach this Play Break, but once they have experienced it, your students will want to play it every day. This game has worked as a Play Break for the early grades through the college level. After a few minutes of playing, your students will be refreshed and ready to get back to their work.

Activity

[Say to students:] I'd like you to find a partner using the following method. Wink with either your left eye or your right eye, and then find another person who is winking with the same eye as you. If you find that you are the only one left winking your left eye, and all the others are winking their right eyes, wink with both eyes and let someone else decide. Now, with your partner, determine who has the most siblings. The person with the most brothers and sisters will begin. If you have the same number of siblings, decide who has the youngest sibling, and that person will begin.

When I say, "Go," I'd like the person who starts first to mime an activity. It could be anything, such as beating eggs in a bowl. It's important for you to perform the physical activity with one hundred percent enthusiasm. Your partner is going to ask you one question and only one question. And that question is: "What are you doing?" Everyone repeat after me: "What are you doing?" Good.

Now, the body and the brain are very sympathetic. If you are pretending to beat eggs in a bowl, you'll automatically want to respond to the question "What are you doing?" by saying, "I'm beating eggs in a bowl." But you must be more clever than that. What you have to think of is a radically different activity from the one you are performing, such as combing your hair. So, as you are beating eggs in the bowl, you are going to say to your partner, "I'm combing my hair." Then you can stop performing your activity.

Your partner must immediately act out the activity you mentioned. He or she starts to comb his or her hair. Then you ask the question "What are you doing?" Your partner has to say anything other than the activity he or she is miming, such as "Washing the dishes." [Set a time limit of one or two minutes for this Play Break.]

137

Example

First person: [Begins miming brushing his/her teeth.]
Second person: What are you doing?
First person: I'm vacuuming the rug.
Second person: [Begins miming vacuuming the rug.]
First person: What are you doing?
Second person: I'm winding my watch.
First person: [Begins miming winding his/her watch.]
Second person: What are you doing?
First person: I'm jump-starting a 747!

Variations

It's okay for students to make up ridiculous or incongruent activities. It's the responsibility of the students' partners to figure out how they are going to mime strange activities, such as "shaving my back" or "climbing to the moon on a rope ladder."

10. Count to Ten!

Overview

This is a very quick Play Break designed to promote cooperation and to build team spirit. Although the game takes less than one minute to complete, the group has a sense of accomplishment when it finally reaches the number ten. You can vary the number of participants, but it's most effective and challenging with ten to twelve students per group.

Activity

[Say to students:] Find two other people, so that you're in a group of exactly three. Now, the three of you find another group of three, so that you form a group of six. Now, the six of you find another group of six, so that you're in a group of twelve. I'd like the group of twelve to form a tight circle, so that you are standing [or sitting] shoulder to shoulder. You are going to count from one to ten. Anyone in your group can start by saying the number one. The idea is for you to count to the number ten, but only one person at a time can speak. You have to listen to succeed with this Play Break. There are two rules. First, if two people say the same number simultaneously, the group has to begin again from the number one. Second, you must count in a random pattern. Don't let one person start with the number one, and the person to the left say the number two, and the next person to the left say three. That's cheating! Keep the counting random and spontaneous. Is everyone ready? Stand shoulder to shoulder or arm in arm if you'd like. Begin now.

Variations

You can create a memory game using this Play Break by substituting information that must be memorized for the counting of numbers. For example, have the group state the first ten presidents in order, the nine planets starting from the sun, the periodic table, the Greek gods or goddesses, or any information that they need to learn.

11. Transform the Object!

Overview

Television has diminished the imaginative abilities of many children. Students, used to seeing ready-made images, have difficulty seeing things that "are not there" or creating unique images. This Play Break stimulates creative thinking and helps students break out of the television "box" they've so readily adopted. Gather a bagful of odd objects from your junk drawer and leave the rest to the imaginations of your students.

Activity

[Place a desk in the center of the room.]

[Say to students:] I need ten volunteers for the Transform the Object Play Break. I'd like five of you to stand on one side of the room and the other five of you to stand on the opposite side of the room. I'm going to take the object from my bag and place it on the desk. Anyone can take an object from the desk and use it in a creative way. To show us how you have transformed the object, you must use it in some way. For example, a tennis ball can become a cigar, a powder puff, a door knob, a candle flame, or a microphone. Let your imaginations soar. Don't let the shape or size of the object limit your ideas. We're going to set a time limit and challenge ourselves to create twenty transformations within two minutes. You cannot hop into the center until the other person has placed the object back on the table. Do you understand the rules? Go! [If you have time, you can have another group of ten come up to play, or you can save this Play Break for another day.]

140

Variations

This can be a verbal Play Break instead of a non-verbal one. Choose three students, and have them stand in the front of the room. They are now "Artifacts Experts." Take an unusual object from your grab bag, and hand it to the students. They must talk about the object as if they were experts.

When one student runs out of things to say about the object, he or she hands it to the next student. The three continue to pass it back and forth, talking about it until their time is up or they run out of things to say. You also can field questions from their classmates if they are having difficulty discussing it.

To make this game more challenging, you can give each person an "area of expertise." These areas could include the historian (gives the background of the object), the engineer (tells how it was made and used), and the psychologist (tells how it affected the people who used it).

I cannot believe that the inscrutable universe turns on an axis of suffering; surely the strange beauty of the world must somewhere rest on pure joy!

– Louise Bogan

12. Let Your Fingers Do the Walking!

Overview

As soon as you mention the word *dance*, many people panic. As we grow older, not only do we move less, we become rigid about the ways in which we move. We rarely move for movement's sake. This nonthreatening Play Break has been very successful with all ages. The idea of this Play Break came from a video about hands and hand movements, which included a jazz pianist performing a complex tap dance with his fingers.

Activity

[Say to students:] Today, we're going to let our fingers do the walking. I'd like you to imagine that two of your fingers are really legs, and they are eager to express themselves. They've been waiting to leap and spin and do the splits. I'd like you to experiment for a few seconds to see what kinds of movements your fingers can make. Can they trip and fall, somersault or limp? I'm now going to play a piece of music [pick age-specific music] for about one minute. Let your fingers do the walking, dancing, and leaping. See what they do.

They are there to entertain you and only you, so concentrate only on what they are doing to the music and not on the other people around you.

Variations

If your students like this Play Break, instead of their fingers, you can have their elbows, knees, noses, toes, or hips do the walking. Play a variety of music, and watch as the hand movements change to match the beat. Try a marching band one time and a rap tune the next. To create a show, collect different kinds of gloves, and have two or three students wear them and spontaneously choreograph a piece in front of the class. Use a place mat or computer mouse mat as a dancing surface for the fingers. For fun, bring in miniature objects that the dancing fingers can use during their movement piece—little rocking chairs, wheelbarrows, boxes, and so forth.

For high school students to feel comfortable with this activity, you might show them a video and ask them to watch the hand movements of the performers. Then have them imitate what they've observed. Make your own video by filming the new hand and finger movements they create.

13. One-Minute Talk

Overview

Many students fear speaking in front of an audience. This Play Break gives students the opportunity to stand up in front of a group and improvise without having to know, remember, or prove anything. It's a great way to help them feel relaxed in front of a group. You can begin by giving a thirty-second time limit and increase it as your students become more comfortable with the form. Every student doesn't need to play every game. Even two or three minutes (two or three students) is plenty of time for your class to become energized. Even if they aren't actively participating, they are no doubt laughing, which is a sign of alertness.

Activity

[Say to students:] I need a volunteer for the One-Minute Talk. Are there any risk takers? Great. We're going to find a subject for you to discuss. Who has an idea? I'm going to write the suggestions on the board [example: peanut butter]. Any other ideas? [Examples: sunburn, washing dishes, skateboarding, the State Fair, and, one more, hamburgers.] Great. I'd like you to choose one of these topics. [Skateboarding.] Okay. Now you have exactly one minute [time this Play Break] to talk about [skateboarding]. You must talk without stopping, except to take a breath. If you run out of things to say, make something up. Use one idea to lead you to the next, but try not to stray from the subject of [skateboards and skateboarding]. Go!

Variations

Once your students feel comfortable with this game, you can add another dimension to it. Slowly increase the amount of time for the students until they can create a complete story—on the spot. You also can use an object such as a cane or wand or Ping-Pong paddle as a "talking stick." The student who holds the talking stick creates a story. When he or she is finished speaking, he or she hands the talking stick to another student, who continues the story. Each student embellishes or adds to the story, trying to keep the plot consistent and the story moving forward. Try using this concept to do a synopsis of a novel your students have finished reading.

143

14. The Forgetful Storyteller

Overview

This verbal Play Break is fast, fun, and hilarious. It requires a high degree of concentration, good listening skills, and an active imagination. It's also a wonderful way to get ideas for creative writing. It would be helpful for you to show the group how to play the Forgetful Storyteller and then have them form pairs so that everyone gets a chance to experience being the Forgetful Storyteller.

Activity

[Say to students:] I'm going to demonstrate this game to you first, and then you'll try it with your partner. First, I'd like you to find a partner. If you are wearing tennis shoes, I'd like you to find someone who is also wearing tennis shoes, and choose that person as your partner. [Use any creative pairing technique.]

I'm going to tell a story, but, unfortunately, I'm a very forgetful storyteller. You'll know I've forgotten where I am in the story because I'll hesitate and repeat things and say "ahhh" a lot. When I hesitate or falter, please assist me by giving me the first word that pops into your head. For example: If I say, "Once upon a . . . upon a . . . ," what word enters your mind? Time? Right! I'll repeat what you said and add it to the story. I'll say, "Time . . . yes . . . once upon a time there was a young . . . a young . . . ahhh . . . " Who has an idea? Goat? A goat. "And this goat was the size of a . . . ," and so forth.

You'll notice that I repeat everything you tell me and then I add it to the story in a way that makes sense. It's my responsibility to make sense of your suggestions and cleverly fit them into the story. My goal is to tell a complete story, with a beginning, middle, and end, within the time limit.

Will you and your partner try this now? The person with the longer hair will begin. You are the Forgetful Storyteller, and your partner fills in the blanks. The more blanks you leave for your partner, the more hilarious your story will be. I'll give you one minute, and then you'll switch and your partner can tell a different story. Are you ready? Okay, begin.

Variations

After the students have practiced leading the story and filling in the blanks, ask a student to come to the front and become the Forgetful Storyteller. The other students fill in the blanks while you act as a scribe to capture the story. Once the story has ended, you can read the storyline back to the Forgetful Storyteller and then have him or her add more depth to the story—setting the scene and adding characters and conflicts. Or you can break the story into chunks and then assign a piece of the story to each student and have each illustrate his or her part. Many classrooms have illustrated stories and books using this technique.

15. Dream a Little Dream With Me!

Overview

Dreaming by day is bound to become a favorite pastime in the 1990s. After all, how can you have a dream come true without first having a dream? This Play Break will expand students beyond their current levels of thinking into the realm of unlimited possibilities where dreams can come true.

Activity

[Say to students:] We're going to take some time to become dreamers by day, and not just when we sleep. Did you know that every great event, idea, and invention began as a dream in someone's imagination? Well, today we are going to imagine a Dream Classroom. Let's close our eyes for a few moments, take a deep breath, and slowly breathe out all of our limited thoughts. Just imagine that they are coming out as a big cloud of smoke. As we do this, we become lighter, and we find ourselves soaring up into the high realms of possibility. The sky is the limit, so let's tap into our creative minds to come up with some outrageous ideas.

There are no right or wrong answers, so let's let ideas flow through our minds without judgment. We are going to put all of our attention on coming up with ideas, rather than commenting on the ideas. We can do that later. Does everybody understand? Great! Let's start with a Dream Teacher. What is he or she like? Let's describe this special person. [Take one or two minutes to generate words and short descriptions, such as "cheerful," "enjoys teaching," and so forth.]

Now, let's create a Dream Student. [Use the same guidelines.] And now, let's describe a Dream Classroom. What does it look like, and what goes on during the day? How long is the school day? How long is the school year? How many of you would like to attend a school like this? How can we make part of this dream come true in our classroom? [Using the ideas that have been generated, brainstorm ways these ideas can be implemented.]

Variations

This Play Break can become a "to be continued" exercise. Try varying the theme to include a Dream Parent, a Dream Friend, a Dream Citizen, a Dream City, a Dream Country, and, finally, a Dream World.

Special Note: We chose to phrase this as *a* Dream Classroom, rather than *the* Dream Classroom, to keep the possibilities open-ended.

26

Notes for Myself

Answers to Wacky Wordies on page 81.

Left to right top:

1. Circles under the eyes.
2. Love at first sight.
3. Standing ovation.
4. That's beside the point!
5. Shape up or ship out!

Left to right bottom:

6. More often than not.
7. Sitting on top of the world.
8. High income bracket.
9. All hands on deck!
10. Jaywalking.

Teaching With Humor That Heals

Part Four

27

The Tribal Tale

Once upon a moment, in a time long forgotten, there lived an ancient people known as the Teehee tribe. They were a rare lot indeed, for they spent their long, carefree days, from sunup until sundown, grinning and laughing. Every morning, to invite the spirit of play into their day, they would smile in each direction and chant:

East is East, and West is West,
To smile each hour will be my test.
North is North, and South is South,
I ask for blessings upon my mouth.

And every evening, to bring peace into the night, they would jump for joy and say:

Now I lay me down to rest,
I ask a grin to be my guest,
And in my dreams perchance I'll see,
That laughter lives, eternally.

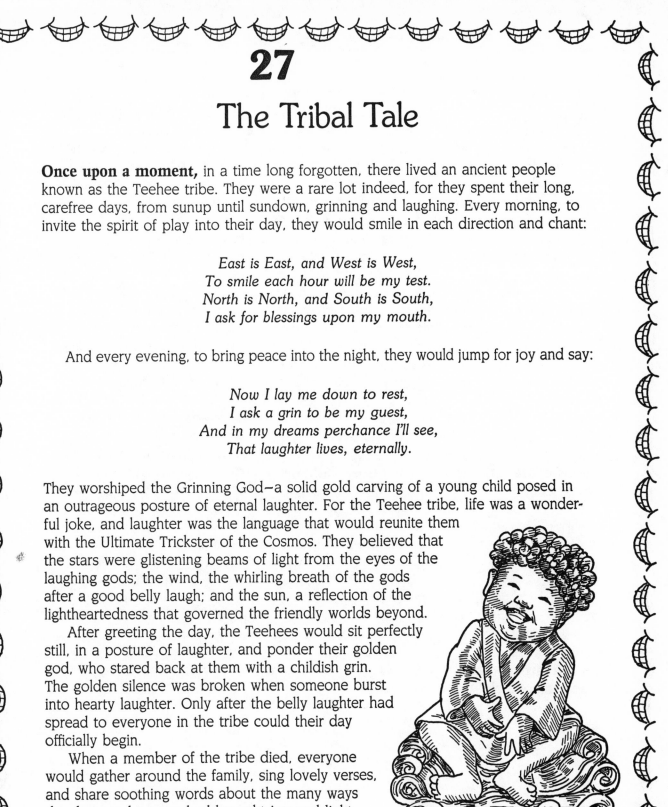

They worshiped the Grinning God—a solid gold carving of a young child posed in an outrageous posture of eternal laughter. For the Teehee tribe, life was a wonderful joke, and laughter was the language that would reunite them with the Ultimate Trickster of the Cosmos. They believed that the stars were glistening beams of light from the eyes of the laughing gods; the wind, the whirling breath of the gods after a good belly laugh; and the sun, a reflection of the lightheartedness that governed the friendly worlds beyond.

After greeting the day, the Teehees would sit perfectly still, in a posture of laughter, and ponder their golden god, who stared back at them with a childish grin. The golden silence was broken when someone burst into hearty laughter. Only after the belly laughter had spread to everyone in the tribe could their day officially begin.

When a member of the tribe died, everyone would gather around the family, sing lovely verses, and share soothing words about the many ways the deceased person had brought joy and lightheartedness to the tribe. This brought the family a great sense of pride, renewal, and peace. When all the family members could smile through their tears, the ashes of the deceased were scattered into the breath of the laughing gods. The soul was now assured a friendly homecoming.

Most curious of all was the way the Teehee tribe raised their young. Their main goal was to raise their children with their "Sol Ra" intact. For the "Sol Ra" (translation: joy that radiates from the inside out) was considered the greatest gift of all. All were born with the laughing "Yes," which was reflected in the toothless grins of their infants. The great quest was to keep this laughing "Yes" from disintegrating into a lackluster "Yes, but . . . " The greatest offense was to grow up and lose sight of "Yes," for it meant the loss of joy. Thus they encouraged their young ones to laugh often. Frequently, a baby's first words were "ha-ha," instead of "ma-ma" or "pa-pa."

On the infrequent occasion when a child misbehaved, the tribe would encircle the child and begin a restorative ritual aiming to breathe the playful spirit back into the child. They believed that the child was suffering from "Solo Nogo" (translation: long face, no smile). This would eventually lead to face ache, a very painful condition because it took many more muscles to frown than to smile.

The face-saving ritual began with buoyant breathing and simultaneous smiling. Everyone inhaled and then exhaled a long series of AHHHHHHHHs, OHHHHHHHHs, and OOOOOOOHs while smiling at the child. This was followed by soft and kind words that acknowledged the child's talents and gifts. When the child began to laugh, the "Solo Nogo" spell was considered broken. Because "Solo Nogo" indicated the deterioration of the child and was considered the root of all disease, the adults would then gather to determine how they might have created an environment where the disease could flourish. Always, their goal was to return the tribe to "glee-quilibrium."

Happiness was the norm, and crime negligible. If one of the adults committed a tribal offense, he or she was sent to a Mirth Maker. The local shaman of silliness determined what was to be done to cure the insensitivity of the culprit. Most were sentenced to spend time crawling on their hands and knees, gurgling and playing with the very young until they regained their spirit of joy and play. Important tribal decisions were never made without a playing baby nearby because the Teehees believed that the presence of a laughing child insured a positive outcome. They had many prayers of thanksgiving and rejoicing. But their most beloved creed, recited by young and old, was simply:

Laugh until you weep,
Weep until you laugh.
Joy is what separates
The wheat from the chaff.

152

28

Teaching With Humor That Heals

There is no question that discipline is a major problem in American schools and in American society today. According to recent research conducted by a leading university in the Midwest, 80 percent of teachers polled claimed that the main problems in their schools involved discipline. Many teachers have left the profession, saying that they decided to become teachers to teach subject matter, not basic manners, and to correct papers, not correct students' attitudes day after day.

Is it possible that a portion of our current discipline problems stems from a serious, heavily regulated approach to the learning process? Oftentimes it's the class clown or the disturbing student that teachers consider to be the biggest discipline problem in the classroom. And yet, the rebel and the class clown both have something significant in common: They refuse to give in to the joyless grind of learning without spontaneity and laughter. Many of their disturbances arise from their innate desire for humor and stimulation in the classroom. This is something that many teachers fail to provide.

Teachers can learn something from behavior-problem students. Outside of the few who suffer from severe problems at home, problem students are often modeling terrific forms of playfulness; the playfulness is just misdirected. Teachers who have taken our courses have commented on a decrease in behavior problems in direct proportion to the addition of humor and play into the classroom.

When the classroom is a lively, creative environment where laughter abounds, students of every age have a natural outlet where their curious minds can flourish. In our experience, a laughing classroom evokes *delightful* forms of play in the learner while a tight-reigned classroom evokes *devious* forms of play (a blend of creativity mixed with rebellion).

Amazingly enough, not even the most stringent environment can extinguish creative play in children and young adults. These qualities are innate in the child. Strict environments do not eliminate playfulness; they simply dictate that playfulness must go "undercover," and thus are born notes, spitballs, paper airplanes, pulled fire alarms, and graffiti. The human brain must create to grow and sustain itself. The creativity process carries its own form of joy. But when creativity is squelched by authoritative control and rote learning, it always comes out sideways, creating a host of bothersome discipline problems.

Clearly, some situations get out of hand and call for an approach that is beyond the use of humor and play in the discipline process. But for the 101 situations that are chronic and predictable, this chapter offers some refreshing new approaches to the energy-draining scenarios that teachers dread. It takes a preventive look at humor and play in the teaching/discipline process and introduces the valuable idea of "replaying."

Although laughter in the classroom is not a cure-all, it can be the grease that turns the axle, the salve that soothes the wound, and the mysterious spark that ignites the flames of true learning, which always includes passionate involvement. Many teachers believe that laughter is an "extra" when it comes to learning. Indeed, they are right. It is an *essential* extra!

29
The Up-Tightrope Test

Directions: The sign of a skillful teacher is the ability to maintain a balance between order and playful abandon. Take this test to discover how well you walk the teacher's tightrope and how often you fly through the day with the greatest of ease.

YES NO

☐ ☐   1. I am able to laugh about small disruptions, but I can nip them in the bud before they become distractions.

☐ ☐   2. I give my students creative, playful outlets during class whenever appropriate.

☐ ☐   3. I am able to make strong directive statements without yelling.

☐ ☐   4. I believe that students who lack self-discipline can learn how to improve their behavior in my classroom.

☐ ☐   5 My students respect me more than they fear me.

☐ ☐   6. I am a good role model for my students. This includes modeling the ability to laugh about my mistakes.

☐ ☐   7. When I become impatient with students, I remind myself that I used to be their age.

☐ ☐   8. I correct students in a firm but positive way.

☐ ☐   9. I choose not to limit my students. A student who misbehaves today might be a shining example of good behavior tomorrow.

☐ ☐ 10. When disciplining students, my demeanor is calm and focused, and I maintain steady eye contact.

☐ ☐ 11. I make it a habit to tell students what I want in the classroom rather than what I don't want.

☐ ☐ 12. I'm enthusiastic and affirming whenever I see positive behavior. I'm an expert at "catching them doing it right."

☐ ☐ 13. I'm able to use my authority without becoming authoritarian.

☐ ☐ 14. I know how to set realistic limits and fair consequences.

☐ ☐ 15. I don't resort to name-calling or put-downs to get the behavior I desire.

☐ ☐ 16. At the end of a difficult day, I am able to put the events of the day into perspective and begin fresh the next morning.

Scoring

Give yourself one point for each *yes* answer.

Acrobatic: 13–16

Congratulations! You have the acrobatic ability to balance concentrated effort with play. Chances are you're considered a star by many of your students and have won the admiration of many of your colleagues. You're able to state your bottom line without the iron net of force and humiliation.

Balanced: 9–12

Your ability to put small annoyances in perspective while stating the rules clearly and fairly gives your classroom a balanced and buoyant tone. Keep up the good balancing act and enthusiastic attitude. The ringmaster is probably very pleased with your performance.

Wobbly: 5–8

Your serious style makes it difficult for you to stay on the rope. Every good tightrope walker knows that in order to stay balanced, you have to relax and "sink into your bones"; otherwise your muscles work against you. Try letting go of the need to control, and you might find yourself having more of it with less effort.

At the End of Your Rope: 1–4

You're hanging on to the rope by one hand, yet you don't realize that you've fallen off. Your approach is hard-nosed and heavy-handed. The rope you walk is the up-tightrope, and it is becoming dangerously frayed. It will surely break, unless you find ways to lighten up and laugh a little. Think about ways to turn your "frayed-knot" rope into a "jump-for-joy" rope.

30

Say It, Replay It!

To say something with humor the first time around is an art form. To "replay" it with humor the second time around is an admirable skill (and, sometimes, a courageous act that garners appreciation). To "replay" a situation is to change an image or word to a more positive image or word. Replaying can be done on the spot, too. Some teachers make it a habit to stop midstream when they catch themselves making a statement that is negative or bleak, and instead they create an "instant replay." This is also a great way to teach students to look at the bright side of a situation. In some classrooms, teachers ask students to do an "instant replay" as well. When this is done in a spirit of play, it can be a powerful tool to teach a vital life skill through the healing power of laughter.

The following Say It, Replay It examples offer some hands-on ways that teachers have chosen to take negative statements and replay them, adding a little bit of lightness for loads of effect.

Say It!	**Replay It!**
1. Stop talking and get to work!	1. Hmmm. If it were quiet in this room right now, I wonder how it would sound.
2. He's a real behavior problem!	2. He really keeps me on my toes!
3. This is the worst class I've ever had!	3. This is a live-wire class! We're all going to learn a lot.
4. The whole family is a mess!	4. The family has been through a lot. They need our encouragement.
5. You are disturbing everyone. What's the matter with you?	5. You can talk as loudly as you like. Just don't use your voice!

6. This school is going downhill!

7. There's way too much to do. We'll never catch up!

8. Thank God, it's Friday!

9. I am really bored with school!

10. If you think he's bad, wait until you get his brother.

11. No one appreciates what I do.

12. You must be out of your mind!

13. The situation is beyond hope.

14.

15. The parents are to blame.

16. I'm so disappointed with your work.

17.

18. This is more work than it's worth!

6. This school needs a face-lift! How can I help?

7. There is much to be done. Let's make it fun!

8. Thank God, it's Monday!

9. I am going to rejuvenate my classroom and lighten up!

10. His little brother is really going to benefit from your help and lightheartedness.

11. I know that I am making a difference.

12. You are a unique thinker!

13. I know there is a solution, and I will find it!

14.

15. The parents need my support and encouragement.

16. I know you are capable of more.

17.

18. I am going to see the humor in this!

| 19. She doesn't have an intelligent bone in her body. | 19. She is full of possibility from head to toe! |
| 20. You will flunk this course if you don't shape up. | 20. You can pass this course if you choose to put forth your best. |

Smile When You "Right" That Six Times!

Here is another approach to "replaying" in the classroom. Teaching seventh-grade social studies, this playful instructor found a humorous way to appeal to his students' funny bone while requesting that they write the following paragraphs six times, depending on the minor offense:

I I will not airmail anything in class because it might be mistaken for a UFO. I realize there's a high probability that it will veer off course and injure a classmate or roll under a desk and turn into a giant teenage mutant litterbug. From now on, I will adopt the motto of the post office and make every effort to hand-deliver the article.

II I will not eat food or chew gum in class because of the likelihood of tooth decay and the possibility that my parents might go bankrupt from my high dental bills. I will not risk the chance of being hypnotized by a gum wad and forced against my will to place it on the side of a desk, underneath a chair, or on my nose.

III This is not a school of beauty, nor is it a barber shop. I will keep all my beauty implements in my purse. Although I value beauty, I will not act like a beast and prop my feet on my classmate's desk to clip my toenails. I understand that the word *cosmetics* comes from the Greek word *kosmos,* and so I'll wait until I'm "outer this space" to handle my hygiene.

With laughter, you can face the unfaceable and erase the unerasable.

31

Before and Laughter Scenarios

Laughter is a universally understood language. Perhaps that is why there is truth in the adage "People who play together, stay together." People dedicated to play surely bond more and build more bridges than they burn. Most of us have experienced moments when mountains have been transformed into molehills through the magical power of laughter and play. Conversely, many people have seen molehills become mountains simply because they lost their levity.

The following Before and Laughter scenarios are identical situations that show the dramatic changes that can happen when laughter is present. In the "Before" scenes, an actual classroom incident is described. In the "And Laughter" scenarios, the same situation is "replayed" using a playful and lighthearted approach.

These stories, although entertaining, are powerful examples of how humor and play can make the quintessential difference in your classroom. Use the stories as a springboard for discussion with your students or peers, or to gain insight into your teaching experiences.

For more insight, recall three highly stressful experiences you have had as an educator. Was humor present in any of these situations? If not, use your imagination to "replay" the scenes and incorporate humor in some fashion. The situations will probably take on a lighter tone. As you reflect upon the following stories, keep our underlying motto in mind: A little bit of play goes a long, long way.

**A heart stretched by a single smile
never goes back to its original dimensions.**

Before

Scene 1: Swim and Sink!

The intermediate swimmers were next in line to take the school swimming test. Today, Suzie regretted that her last name began with the letter A. She wished she had stayed home and feigned sickness. She felt confident about everything but the first diving event. As she approached the diving board and glanced at her swimming coach's stern face, she noticed she was short of breath. Coach Hendrich impatiently said, "Let's move it along, Andrews. We don't have all day. There are other students waiting to dive, you know."

Suzie closed her eyes, extended her arms, and dove into the uninviting cold water. To her horror, she landed with a loud splash, belly first. Her embarrassment and anguish were apparent as she swam to the side of the pool. She sheepishly greeted her snickering class-  mates with a reddened face while looking to Coach Hendrich for reassurance. The coach was serious and tense. He quickly nodded his head back and forth in a gesture of disapproval and said, "Go to the flukes' line, Andrews." Humiliated, Suzie got out of the water, dreading the second try that she'd be asked to make. Why had she agreed to take this class in the first place? Her mom couldn't dive. What made her think that she could learn?

During her second dive, Suzie's knees shook so much that she didn't take the time to stand up straight before leaping off the diving board. She wanted to get it over so that she could go home, hide under the covers, and stay away from pools for the rest of her life. This time, she plunged sideways into the pool, splashing a few of the observers in the front row. As she came up for air, the coach gave her the thumbs-down motion, saying, "Out, Andrews. Try it again next year, huh? Oh, and next time, bring some towels for the front row." He chuckled under his breath.

Suzie got out of the water shivering and ashamed, glad that her mom had to work and wasn't there to see her fail. "Never again," she said to herself over and over as she dried off in the shower room. "Swimming isn't for me. . . ."

Suzie kept her vow and refused to take the intermediate class. Thirty-five years later, Suzie is still a novice swimmer. She swims just enough to do slow sidestrokes or backstrokes a few times a year. Her husband is an avid swimmer who swims three times a week at the YMCA. When he's asked why his wife never joins him, he replies, "Oh, swimming isn't for her. She just never quite got the hang of it."

. . . And Laughter

Replay of Scene 1: You'll Float No Matter What!

The intermediate swimmers were next in line to take the school swimming test. Since Suzie's last name began with the letter A, she knew that she'd be the first one to dive. She felt confident about everything but the diving, which had been her greatest challenge during class. Suzie approached the diving board. She glanced at her swimming coach's smiling face and took a deep breath, as he had taught them to do when they were nervous. "Go for it, Suzie," Coach Hendrich said encouragingly. Suzie grinned at him as she extended her arms and dove into the uninviting cold water.

To her surprise, she landed in the water with a loud splash, belly first. She could feel her face getting red before she got to the side of the pool. As she stepped out of the pool, she glanced at Coach Hendrich, who reassured her by giving her a pat on the back. She noticed some of her classmates were giggling. "Even fish dive belly first sometimes, Suzie," the coach said. "Do you see that line over there? That's called the fun line. It's for swimmers like you who think it's so much fun the first time, they just can't wait to do it a second time!" Suzie chuckled and said, "Yeah, right, Coach!"

Despite the coach's positive words, Suzie wondered if her second dive would be better. After all, her mother never learned to dive. Maybe it just wasn't one of her talents. As she stood, ready to dive again, Hendrich shouted, "Keep it light, Andrews. Breathe slowly, lower your arms a little, and *smile!*" She smiled at him, but this time dove too fast and landed with another belly flop. She felt herself laugh underwater, wondering what her coach would say this time about her less-than-perfect performance. Chagrined, Suzie surfaced, knowing that she'd have to start over next semester.

"Well, Suzie, I guess you just can't get enough of me. Next semester, you'll pass with flying colors! This summer, whenever you swim, practice your diving steps. Next year, you'll be diving like a dolphin." Her coach looked at her and, with a gleam in his eyes, winked. "Diving like a dolphin," Suzie repeated to herself during her swimming practice sessions. All summer, she pretended to be a dolphin.

Grief can take care of itself, but to get the full value of a joy, you must have someone to divide it with. – Mark Twain

Suzie passed the intermediate class the following semester, plus the divers' class and the lifesavers' class within a year. Thirty-five years later, Suzie is an avid swimmer. She swims three times a week at the YMCA with her husband. "It's great aerobic exercise," Suzie says to convince her friends to join her. She has a large glass statue of a dolphin in her living room. "Dolphins are my favorite animal. I don't know why I like them so much—maybe it's their gracefulness."

**By the power of your laugh,
a whole is made from half.**

Before

Scene 2: The Books Are Dropping!

It was Miss Baker's first day as a two-week substitute teacher for a sixth-grade class, which, according to the principal, "was a challenging and unruly bunch." She was determined to maintain some semblance of order, no matter what. The students were also determined—determined to show her as soon as possible who was running the show.

At recess, Billy, the classroom leader, hatched a plan with his friends. By the end of the recess period, everyone had "passed it on." "Remember," Billy said as the bell rang, "the first time she turns her back, we all count to three and then drop our books on the floor. That oughta rattle her cage!"

Soon after the class began, Miss Baker turned her back to write on the board. Billy, with a devilish grin on his face, silently counted to three. One, two, three . . . WHAM! Thirty-six English textbooks fell in amazing unison.

Miss Baker, startled by the loud sound, tensed her shoulders and dropped her chalk. She could feel the hair on the back of her neck rise as snickering filled the room. She wondered what she should do. She definitely didn't want this disruptive behavior to continue during the next two weeks.

She turned around, her face reddened with anger, and said with clenched teeth, "Very clever. Your teacher didn't tell me that you worked so well as a team. I hope you'll be just as successful at reading the extra chapter that I'm assigning tonight. Maybe you can organize a study group." She put down her chalk and looked smugly at the bewildered and embarrassed students. "I'll be testing you tomorrow just to assure that you've done what I've asked. Oh, and if this should happen again, I'll make sure to give you an even longer assignment."

The moment she looked away, Billy began making faces at her. Several students started shifting in their seats, wondering if they could find time to finish the extra assignment. The rest of the afternoon dragged. Half of the class was listless, and the other half was fidgety. Miss Baker, although drained, was relieved that she had put them in their place so quickly. At 3:10 P.M., the long-awaited bell finally rang.

"What a witch," Billy mumbled under his breath as he stepped out of the classroom. "Yeah. I can't wait until our two-week prison term is over," his friend replied, rolling his eyes.

Miss Baker drove home with a headache, wondering about the chapter test she would have to create for the next day. Meanwhile, her listless and fidgety students were at home trying to keep their eyes open as they begrudgingly studied the extra chapter.

"Kids these days are so out of control," Miss Baker said to herself as she pulled into her driveway.

. . . And Laughter

Replay of Scene 2: The Sub Is Hopping!

It was Miss Baker's first day as a two-week substitute for a very lively sixth-grade class. Despite the warning she had received from the school principal, she was determined to keep two primary goals in mind while she was teaching. The first was to maintain order, and the second was to have an enjoyable time together. The sixth-grade class had just one goal—to show her who was really running the show.

Billy, one of the classroom leaders, hatched a plan with his friends during recess. By the end of recess, everyone had "passed it on." "Remember," he said as the bell rang, "when she turns her back, I'll signal, and on the count of three, we'll all drop our books. That oughta rattle her cage!"

Soon, Miss Baker turned her back to write on the board. Billy silently counted to three. One, two, three . . . WHAM. Thirty-six textbooks fell to the floor in amazing unison. Miss Baker, startled, tensed her shoulders and dropped the chalk. She could feel the hair on the back of her neck rise as snickering resounded throughout the room. She wondered what she should do. She definitely didn't want this disruptive behavior to continue over the next few weeks.

Her mind raced as she stood with her back to her students for what seemed to be the longest ten seconds of silence in the history of public education. She reminded herself of her two major goals—to maintain order and to have fun. Aha! A brilliant idea suddenly came to mind. Her face lightened, and her shoulders relaxed. As she whirled around to face her smug students, she reached for her textbook and knocked it off the desk and onto the floor, where it landed with a loud thud. "Sorry I'm a little late," she retorted. With a grin she added, "Next time you'll have to give me fair warning."

Billy's jaw dropped in disbelief. Students squirmed in their seats and glanced at one another, unsure of what to do next. Miss Baker laughed aloud, which was quickly echoed by the class. "I love a good laugh," she said. "In the future, just let me in on it, okay?" The tension dissipated. Miss Baker had won them over. The rest of the afternoon went smoothly and was filled with lively discussion. Even Billy answered a few of her questions. At 3:10, the bell rang. Several students dawdled momentarily to talk with Miss Baker.

"She's not bad," commented one of Billy's cronies as they walked out of the room. "We'll see," said Billy. "Maybe there is a good apple in the bunch."

Miss Baker drove home feeling energized. She had established rapport and order in one "fell swoop" of a textbook—plus a lifetime of working hard to find the balance between the two. Meanwhile, her delighted students went home and talked about their unusual new substitute.

"Kids these days are pretty neat," Miss Baker said to herself as she pulled into her driveway.

Before

Scene 3: Give Me That Note, She Said With a Gloat!

Rebecca discreetly passed a note across the aisle to her friend Marley. Before Marley could reach it, Ms. Bentov interceded from behind the two girls and snatched the note out of Marley's hand. "Is this how you use your study time, Rebecca?" Ms. Bentov stood over Rebecca's desk

with her arms crossed, tapping her foot. "It's about our girl scout meeting tonight," Rebecca answered quickly. "I don't care what it's about, Rebecca! You've just earned your third check on the blackboard," Ms. Bentov said as she walked briskly to the blackboard and put another check after the name Rebecca Sanborn. "It looks like you won't be going to girl scouts after school tonight. You'll be serving a detention instead."

Rebecca sank down in her seat and gave Marley a bewildered look. Some of her classmates sneered at her, while others looked down steadfastly at their work, hoping that they wouldn't be the next ones to get a dreaded check mark. Rebecca gave Ms. Bentov a scornful glance. She hated the embarrassment of having her name on the board with three check marks after it. She could feel her face beginning to burn as she stared down at her desk.

"A few of you have two marks after your names. Stick to your work, or you'll be serving detention with Rebecca after school today," Rebecca heard her teacher say. The room was very still for the remainder of the class, but Rebecca could no longer concentrate on her work. "It's not fair," she kept telling herself. "It was just a note about the meeting." What would she tell her troop leader? She was the head of the cookie committee, and today she was in charge of an important meeting. She swallowed hard, trying to push down the thick lump forming in her throat. "I hate her," she said to herself. "I can't wait until I'm out of here," she thought, as she watched the clock

. . . And Laughter

Replay of Scene 3: Write With All Your Might!

Rebecca discreetly passed a note across the aisle to her friend Marley. Before Marley could reach it, Ms. Bentov interceded from behind the two girls. "Aha! A free-floating letter making its way to an avid recipient. Well, it will have to wait until after class, Rebecca," Ms. Bentov said with a smile as she gestured for the note with her outstretched hand. "We are a classroom, not a post office, girls. I'll keep the note for you until the bell rings." Marley handed the note to her teacher, as Rebecca responded by saying, "But it's about our girl scout meeting tonight, Ms. Bentov."

"And I'm sure that the urgency of this matter just couldn't wait until the bell rang?" Ms. Bentov asked, tongue-in-cheek. "Well, I guess it can wait," Rebecca said with a sheepish grin.

"I'm sure it can, Rebecca. Because this has happened

twice this week, it seems to me that we have a little problem on our hands. One of our classroom agreements, if you'll recall, was not to pass notes during class. I have an idea. Why don't you take your talent and interest in writing notes and create a clever note written to the class about the five benefits of *not* writing notes in class? You can make it as funny and entertaining as you like, but I want you to find five good reasons."

"Do I have to?" Rebecca replied with a grimace.

"I can't think of a better way to cure your classroom cravings for note writing, Rebecca. Please bring it to class next Monday." Ms. Bentov walked back to the front of the room, smiling. Rebecca stared at the clock for a few minutes. She already had thought of some funny ideas she'd include in her class note. She'd make it entertaining, as Ms. Bentov had suggested, but she decided she would stop passing notes in class so she wouldn't have to create another five reasons for not writing notes in school.

Before

Scene 4: Get Ready, Get Set, Oh No!

Hundreds of college freshmen eagerly filed into the large Anatomy/Physiology 101 lecture hall. It was the largest classroom many had ever seen.

"Hello, my name is Jenny," a young woman said to the student next to her. "Do you know what Professor Cantor is like?"

"No, I don't, but I hope he's not tough. I have a full load this semester and a part-time job. By the way, my name is Robert."

"Attention please," the professor sternly said from the lecture platform. "I'd like to welcome you to Anatomy/Physiology 101. I'm Professor Cantor. Let me preface today's lecture by saying that this course will be the most difficult course you'll take at this university."

Jenny felt her heart sink as she glanced at Robert, who stared ahead and listened intently.

"I'm going to see to it that you are challenged the way a college student should be challenged. You will be taking an extensive test each week. I'll expect you to read two chapters per week. The questions will be difficult, and to answer them successfully you'll have to know the material as well as you know your social security number."

Robert glanced at Jenny. Professor Cantor continued. "Just for your

ANATOMY/ PHYSIOLOGY 101

enrollment-
500 - now
400 - in 3 weeks
300 or less } in 3 months

information, there are about five hundred students registered for this course. Within three weeks, at least one hundred of you will drop out. You see, by making this class challenging and difficult, I can quickly weed out the motivated learners from the bench warmers. College isn't a place for bench warmers, as you'll soon learn. After three months, one hundred more students will be gone. That means that forty percent of the people seated here today will not be with us by April. Look around the room. Will you be one of them? Yes, it's a high dropout rate, but, believe me, you'll know your physiology when you leave this course.

And you'll know the meaning of hard work and accomplishment. Well, I've spoken my piece. Do you have any questions?"

Yes, Jenny wondered to herself. Were there any other freshman science classes left with openings? She turned to ask Robert, but he was no longer in his seat. At that moment, Jenny knew that it would be a long semester.

Humor works by rallying, and by being a manifestation of, the will to live.
— Dr. Raymond Moody, Jr.

169

. . . And Laughter

Replay of Scene 4: Get Ready, Get Set, Let's Go!

Hundreds of college freshmen eagerly filed into the large Anatomy/Physiology 101 lecture hall, chuckling as they looked at the blackboard. "LET'S GET PHYSICAL" was written in large letters, with a whimsical drawing of a professor examining a skeleton. "Hi, I'm Jenny," said a young woman to the student seated next to her. "Have you heard anything about Professor Cantor?" "No, I haven't, but I hope he's not tough. I'm already carrying a full load this semester. Incidentally, my name is Robert."

"Attention, please," a cheerful voice announced from the lecture platform. "Welcome to Anatomy/Physiology 101. I'm Professor Cantor." The students turned their attention to the front of the room and began to laugh and whisper to each other. Professor Cantor was dressed in a nineteenth-century costume and wore a clown wig. He stood next to a life-size skeletal model that hung on a metal stand.

"You've heard the phrase 'A picture is worth a thousand words'? Well, my outfit today illustrates my philosophy of education and my teaching style. I believe in the old-fashioned rules about school: Work them to the bone, until they really have it in their blood. Right, Alfred?" He shook the hand of his skeleton friend, causing a wave of laughter to ripple through the room. "But," he mused, "because you prevent them from feeling *grave* about

ANATOMY/
PHYSIOLOGY
101

Let's get
physical!

the work, they begin to *dig* what they're learning," Professor Cantor said while scratching his clown wig. The students chuckled.

"You'll be tested weekly in this course—two chapters per week. If you'll hold up your end of the agreement, I promise to hold up mine. You show up, study hard, and come to class with all the questions that your minds can muster, and I'll provide the information, the inspiration, and the entertainment, all in one. Deal?"

"Deal," replied the energized freshmen.

"They'll know anatomy and physiology *inside out* when they're done in this class, right, Alfred?" The students began to laugh. "By the way, Alfred is an old student of mine who insists on hanging around with me every semester, so I have made him my teaching assistant," the professor said as he rested Alfred's bony hand on his shoulder. The group burst into laughter as Professor Cantor stood posing arm in arm with Alfred.

"Just for your information, because of the university's fire code, you won't be allowed to invite other students to attend our class. When you tell your friends that you're having so much fun with a topic as challenging as this, they'll be skeptical and want to come to see for themselves. But because we are filled to capacity, you'll just have to give them the bare bones yourself. By the end of this course, you'll know the meaning of hard work, but you'll also know the meaning of a good belly laugh. Through group interaction, comedy, skits, and other essential nonsense, you'll be able to recite this material in your sleep. You might even start whispering sweet anatomical nothings into your sweetheart's ear at night." The group chuckled. "Except Alfred, of course. He doesn't sleep anymore. He gave it up a while ago. In fact, he doesn't eat either. That's why he's just a bag of bones!"

Jenny laughed aloud, and then smiled at Robert. At that moment, she knew that the course would end far too soon and that Professor Cantor would be an instructor she'd remember for a long, long time.

And they lived happily ever laughter!

171

32

Fifty Ways to Say You Did Okay

We bet that your own possibilities give you goosebumps!

1. Three cheers!
2. Good for you!
3. Gold medal performance!
4. Celebrate your success!
5. Super job!
6. Thumbs up once again!
7. WOW!
8. Onward and upward!
9. A-1 achievement!
10. Keep up the terrific work!
11. Thanks for the lift!
12. Five-star rating!
13. Reward yourself!
14. You must be proud of yourself!
15. Intelligence strikes again!
16. Splendid success!
17. I appreciate your effort!
18. Your mind is a work of art!
19. You're an exception to the rule!
20. Nice going!
21. Give yourself a standing ovation!
22. First-class all the way!
23. You're amazing!
24. You just keep getting better!
25. Hats off to you!
26. You have a winning attitude!
27. Pat yourself on the back!
28. Marvelous contribution!
29. Unforgettable!
30. You deserve a lot of credit!
31. Quality is your middle name!

32. Can I have your autograph?
33. Positively peak performance!
34. It's obvious that you care!
35. Unbelievably well done!
36. Do it again!
37. You'll inspire others!
38. I admire what you've done!
39. Exceptional!
40. You're destined for greatness!
41. What know-how!
42. Your brilliance never ceases to amaze me!
43. Nothing's impossible for you!
44. You always do your best!
45. You've gone that extra mile!
46. You've exceeded my expectations!
47. Congratulations! Let me give you a hug!
48. Exemplary!
49. You really met the challenge!
50. Your potential is showing!

It's a privilege to watch a genius in the making!

33
$\textcircled{A+}$ Exceptional Excuses $\textcircled{A+}$

You've probably heard just about every lamebrain excuse in the book. But as you will see, there's a never-ending supply due to the brain's creativity. If a student doesn't finish an assignment or requests an extension, have him or her fill out this Exceptional Excuses sheet. Or create your own.

❝ I would have completed my homework but . . . ❞

☐ My computer was down.

☐ I feel that my brilliance exempts me from this fruitless labor. I am going to write my own text as an alternative.

☐ My dog was really sick and fell asleep right on my schoolbooks, and my mom was afraid that the dog might throw up on the clean rug if I woke him up.

☐ I'm in need of a student time-management course, *fast!*

☐ I haven't been able to save up enough money to pay my brother to write my papers.

☐ I know that I have a really good reason . . . I just can't remember what it is! Maybe if I'm given a month's vacation, I'll remember.

☐ My father says I don't have to do it, and father knows best.

☐ I didn't finish dinner last night, and my mom wouldn't let me leave the table to do my homework.

☐ I got lost underneath my covers, and nobody found me until it was too late to do my assignments.

☐ The phone kept ringing all night, and because no one else was home I was forced to answer it.

34

Song: "Nifty Ways to Learn by Laughing"

This song is sung to the Paul Simon tune.

If dread is hidden in your hearts, as I've been told,
Or if your love for school has changed from hot to cold,
I'll share the alchemy that turns a heart to gold.
There must be nifty ways to learn by laughing,
Nifty ways to learn by laughing.

Just laugh 'til you ache, Jake. Make yourself sane, Jane.
Fill up to the brim, Tim. Just giggle with me.
It starts with a smile, Kyle. Try it out for a short while.
Just choose to have joy, Roy. You'll see it's the key.

If school's not fulfilling, and you're sure you've had enough,
If just trying to survive has made you really tough,
There's a way to smooth the edges that are rough.
There are some nifty ways to learn by laughing,
Nifty ways to learn by laughing.

Don't choose to feel bad, Brad. Say, "Yes, I can," Nan.
You're not in a race, Grace. Do an about-face.
You're on the right track, Jack. There's no reason to turn back.
Be a Cheshire cat, Matt, and not commonplace.

If hope is gone, and you are feeling worse for wear,
Remember that once upon a time you used to care.
There is a playful answer I would like to share:
There are some nifty ways to learn by laughing,
Nifty ways to learn by laughing.

Make your grin wide, Clyde. Don't appear grave, Dave.
Why make yourself sick, Dick? Just imitate me.
Just lose your distress, Bess. Don't give it a second guess.
Take time to be jolly, Molly. 'Cause laughter is free.

Show all your teeth, Keith. It's okay to play, Kay.
Make chuckling a goal, Joel. It's very easy.
Open your heart, Bart. Just give it a jump-start.
You'll see a new spark, Mark. You've our guarantee!

35
Humor Homework

1. Practice using an empty frame as a prop whenever you need to *reframe* a negative statement.

2. Smile often in class. Keep a mirror on your desk as a reminder to take yourself lightly even though you take your job seriously.

3. When a problem arises, take a mental vow to keep it in perspective. Ask yourself if it will really matter one month or one year from now.

4. Become aware of those instances where you automatically use sarcasm and ridicule instead of humor that heals. Log them in a book until the time when you can catch yourself before you speak.

5. Choose either one Warm-up, one Play Break, or one Laughing Lesson, and implement it in your next teaching session. Keep a log of your results.

36

Play Sheet

1. When you were a child, how did you feel about learning?

2. What is one of the most valuable things that you learned in school?

3. What was your opinion about school? List your various grade levels and your corresponding opinion about school. Write your reasons for any significant change of opinion about school you might have had.

4. List three things that you would like to see changed in your school.

5. List three things you appreciate about your school.

6. What is the greatest gift you can give to your students?

37
Notes for Myself

Using Laughter Forever After

Part Five

38

Through the Laughing Glass

He was always happy, despite being surrounded by adults who were not. They walked quickly, told him what to do and exactly how to do it, and were forever talking at him or looking through him. But it didn't matter because he'd run through the meadow and sing for no reason at all, then carve his smile in the clouds. He'd lie on the cool grass and gaze at the sky, and only the sun, the sky, and the clouds heard what he was saying.

One sunny day, he created a laugh for no reason at all. It started as a giggle, then, after slowly growing into a guffaw, it made a beeline for his belly and burst forth from him with such power that the heavens and earth shook. Oh, it was a glorious sound, the laugh! It became a secret between him and the sun, the sky, and the clouds. At night, when he was alone and he closed his eyes, he could still hear it. The laugh was his friend, and he loved it.

When he started school, he was happy. Now he could share the laugh. He could run, shout, and sing with others, for no reason at all. But it was a funny school, in a serious sort of way. He had to sit up straight at his desk, with his arms still, his eyes forward, and his feet stiff and flat on the floor. He wanted to jump and laugh and run and play. But he was instructed to "walk in a line, hold the pencil straight, don't

181

talk, don't touch, mind your manners, don't turn around, don't make a sound, sit up, keep your eyes on your work, raise your head, listen to directions, and have a nice day."

He tried to follow all the new rules, but it was most difficult. He wanted to sway like the trees in the wind when he walked down the aisles. He ached to touch the soft rabbit behind the glass cage labeled "Do not touch." He longed to tumble and laugh with the other children who were trying ever so hard to hold their heads still and their pencils straight and keep their feet flat on the floor.

One afternoon, so as not to die of dullness, he made a sound like an owl. His teacher gave him a gray slip to take home that read, "He is disturbing others for no reason at all. You must teach him to behave." After that, he did his best to sit up straight, mind his manners, and never hoot like an owl, chirp like a cricket, or make fish faces at his friends. Everything that made him happy he kept hidden inside. His teacher sent home a yellow note that read, "Big improvement. He's learning to do what he is told." Now he was totally confused. Whenever he felt bright and cheerful, like the color yellow, he got a gray slip. Whenever he felt bored and tired, like the color gray, he got a yellow slip. School was a puzzling place.

One morning, when he was sure that he would burst from boredom, it happened. The laugh accidentally slipped out while his teacher was writing on the blackboard. It began quietly, but when it moved into his belly, it became so big that it burst forth, making the floors and ceiling shake. "What's so funny? Would you like to share it with everyone else? Foolish young man, do you think that life is one big joke?" his teacher said, sending him home with a gray slip that read, "He laughs for no reason at all. Do something immediately, or he will be suspended." His parents told him to behave and do what his teacher said he should do.

His teacher moved his desk into a corner, away from everyone. After that, he did as he was told, and he followed all the rules, no matter how confusing they seemed. His only consolation was a small window near his lonely corner. When he turned his body, just so, he could catch a glimpse of the sun, the sky, and the clouds. He knew they shared a secret. Whenever he looked through the window and saw them, he was happy, for he remembered the secret that they shared.

And as he sat, still and stiff, he thought about his secret. The window became his laughing glass, his passage into a world where all of his thoughts and feelings were heard. "I know what I'm going to be when I grow up," he told the sun, the sky, and the clouds. "I'm going to be a *foolish* teacher, and my students will run through meadows, sing for no reason at all, and carve their smiles in the clouds!" The sun beamed at him through the laughing glass, and the clouds replied, "You are a wonderful boy. Soon you will grow up and share our simple secret: Joy . . . for no reason at all!"

39
Using Laughter Forever After

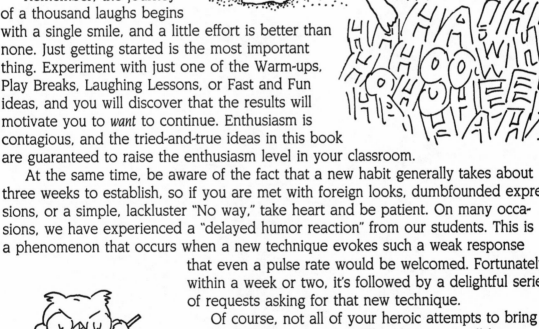

By now, you are probably leaping with enthusiasm over the power of using laughter and play in the classroom or, at the very least, enchanted with a few of the new ideas you've learned. We commend your playful efforts and encourage you to continue to use the techniques and ideas in the book, as well as adapting the ones that you have enjoyed.

Remember, the journey of a thousand laughs begins with a single smile, and a little effort is better than none. Just getting started is the most important thing. Experiment with just one of the Warm-ups, Play Breaks, Laughing Lessons, or Fast and Fun ideas, and you will discover that the results will motivate you to *want* to continue. Enthusiasm is contagious, and the tried-and-true ideas in this book are guaranteed to raise the enthusiasm level in your classroom.

At the same time, be aware of the fact that a new habit generally takes about three weeks to establish, so if you are met with foreign looks, dumbfounded expressions, or a simple, lackluster "No way," take heart and be patient. On many occasions, we have experienced a "delayed humor reaction" from our students. This is a phenomenon that occurs when a new technique evokes such a weak response that even a pulse rate would be welcomed. Fortunately, within a week or two, it's followed by a delightful series of requests asking for that new technique.

Of course, not all of your heroic attempts to bring more laughter and joy into the classroom will be met with initial resistance. In fact, we predict that most of the time the new techniques will evoke such a favorable response that the giggles and reverberations will surprise even you! Students will talk to their friends about what they are learning in school, and they will even go

The most completely lost of all days is that on which one has not laughed. – Chamfort

home talking about how much fun they've had at school. Parents may begin calling and writing to acknowledge your efforts, and curious colleagues will take notice and begin to pick your brain in the teachers' lounge or even come in to observe some of the successful silliness for themselves.

But these are just a few of the side benefits that may accompany your efforts. The real rewards will return to you in renewed vigor for teaching, a closer rapport with students, and a pleasant tone of playfulness in the atmosphere that will evoke more student involvement than you dreamed possible—not to mention test scores that will cause even the cold and stone faced to sit up and take notice.

So take heart, laughing teacher, and remember that a few laughs a day keeps the classroom blahs away. This last section will serve as a playful reminder that life has its comic moments if you take the time to see them. May you stay forever young as you embark upon your playful journey, using laughter forever after.

It's your "laughitude," not your aptitude,
that determines your altitude.

40

Let's Get Quizzical: A Humor Questionnaire

Directions: Here is a quick quiz for you, "Teach," to help you determine whether you have a good, bad, or non-sense of humor. You will be awarded points for your answers and judged with extreme sensitivity according to fair, impartial biases. Thank you for your "fluidity" in this matter. You may begin.

Name _____

Address _____

Telephone ( ) _____ Age _____ Attention Span _____

Vital Statistics: Height _____ Weight _____ Depth _____

Monthly Income _____ Monthly Outgo _____

Please Check ✔ the Correct Answer.

Example: Is the word *weather* spelled correctly in the first paragraph?

☐ **YES**   ☐ **NO**

YES	NO	
☐	☐	1. Do you have a classroom?
☐	☐	2. Do you have a sense of humor?
☐	☐	3. Do you have a sense of humor about your classroom?
☐	☐	4. If you don't have one, would you like to find one?
☐	☐	5. Do you believe puns are the lowest form of humor?
☐	☐	6. Do you think there's laughter in the hereafter?
☐	☐	7. Do you have a class clown?
☐	☐	8. Are you the class clown?
		Do you like silly visual jokes¿ ☐ Yes ☐ No 9.
☐	☐	10. Do you know who said, "Don't worry, be haphazard"?
☐	☐	11. Have you had your bad temper shots?
☐	☐	12. Can you spare a teacher a quarter for a cup of coffee?
☐	☐	13. Did you know that no one has died from too much laughter?
☐	☐	14. Do you laugh so hard that you shake, rattle, and roll on the floor?
		15. Have you read:
☐	☐	• *A Funny Thing Happened on the Way to the Teachers' Lounge?*
☐	☐	• *The One-Minute Laffer?*

Connect the Punch Line.

16. Why did the teacher buy bifocals?
17. What happens when principals retire?
18. Why are kindergarten teachers special?
19. What happens when you stifle laughter?
20. How is self-deprecating humor like history?
21. Why don't man-eating lions eat clowns?

a. They lose their faculties.
b. They know how to make the little things count.
c. It moves down your body and starts to expand your hips.
d. They taste funny.
e. She had bad pupils.
f. It repeats itself way too often.

22. Circle the words that best describe your special brand of humor.

Automatic	Woofed	Idiotic	Schtick
Caustic	Spoofed	Biting	Drollish
Sarcastic	Analogous	Teething	Droolish
Bombastic	Anomalous	Playful	Foolish
Comical	Analytical	Zany	Clean
Anatomical	Punster	Brainy	Nonexistent
Trivial	Dumpster	Antediluvian	Nonchalant
Pedantic	Passable	Antebellum	None of your
Varied	Wholesome	Antacid	beeswax
Harried	"Halfsome"	Ribald	
Original	Deadpan	"Riboflavinous"	
Marginal	Bedpan	Intravenous	
"Migrainal"	Antiseptic	Heinous	
Irrational	Peptic	Genius	
Irascible	Mechanistic	Tongue in	
Jovial	Futuristic	Cheek	
Juvenile	Convoluted	Tongue in	
Slapstick	Polluted	Groove	
Purulent	Raw	Dry	
Perverse	Parboiled	Moist	
Pernicious	Cosmic	Quick	
Delicious	Laconic	Sick	
Warped	Exotic	Slick	

Fill in the Blanks.
(Please keep your classroom in mind.)

23. Laugh and the whole _____ laughs with you.

24. What if I _____ in the middle of your _____ ?

25. Did you hear that _____ and _____ are _____ ?

26. _____ ! _____ _____ _____ _____ money!

27. Please check if you have the following:

	Glaringly Obvious	Slightly Visible	I'm Not Saying
Tupperware Brain Syndrome			
"Humorrhoids"			
Terminal Tightness			
Mental Mush Disease			
Wonder Dread			
Acute Maturation			
Nervous Twitches			
Fainting Spells			
Magic Spells			
Harrowing Experiences			
Narrowing Viewpoints			

Please Circle the Correct Answer.

28. Do you use humor to
    a) escape reality?
    b) bond and cement?
    c) lose weight?
29. To whom do you owe your sense of humor?
    a) Your father and mother
    b) The good humor man
    c) The IRS
30. What do you do for fun?
    a) Answer questionnaires
    b) Duplicate your efforts
    c) Take extra sick days
31. Should laughter be encouraged?
    a) Yes
    b) None of the above
    c) All of the above
32. Where do you remain the most often?
    a) In your adult
    b) In your parent
    c) In your head
33. How intense are your "mirth-quakes"?
    a) All my students crack up.
    b) I have no-fault insurance.
    c) I haven't been able to "fissure" it out.

34. Who said, "I like children—well-done!"
    a) W. C. Fields
    b) Julia Child
    c) Those who have had them
35. Which do you prefer?
    a) Belly laughs
    b) Belly rolls
    c) A different job
36. What makes you uncomfortable?
    a) Indoor recess
    b) Deciding what to wear to work
    c) Varicose veins
37. When you're teaching do you
    a) chortle and chuckle?
    b) twitter and titter?
    c) rock and roll?
38. Is your favorite funny expression
    a) "I like moderation in excess"?
    b) "I'm in favor of existential sten-cils"?
    c) "I'm glad you asked me that question"?
39. Where did laughter originate?
    a) The small intestines
    b) The primordial fireball
    c) Kansas

Essay Questions
Be as unclear and verbose as you can.

40. In two words or less, please describe what you perceive your comic destiny to be.

41. What was Hamlet's major flaw?

42. What is your major flaw?

43. Where is the funny bone located, and how do you tickle it?

44. Bonus Question: Compare and contrast Mesopotamian obscurantist humor with the compendious humor of Mark Twain.

SCORING

Give yourself one point for each question that you have answered.

61 or up	Impossible to score this high.
30–44	**Unbelievable:** You need to moonlight as a stand-up comic.
19–29	**Humorosity Maximus:** Perfect in every respect. You could be a teacher!
10–18	**Humorosity Middlemus:** You have a foot in both worlds. Wear stretch pants.
1–9	**Humorosity Minimus:** You lack the basic skills. Pursue bill collecting as a hobby.
Under 1	**Deplorable:** Check your pulse. Are you sure you're alive?

41
Ask Ann Laffers!

Letter 1

Dear Ann,
    I have thirty-five students in my class-room, and most of them are borderline hyperactive. I'm afraid that if I get them laughing, they won't be able to stop and I'll lose what little control I now have. What do you suggest I do?
        Just sign me,
        Wired and
        Worried

Ann Replies

Dear Wired,
    Children who are hyperactive have shorter attention spans and become easily distracted. Those children, in turn, distract other children, and before you know it, the entire class is oper-ating on their wavelength. Believe it or not, humor can help to settle down a class like yours. If you plan your Play Breaks, *you'll* be in control, not the children who are misbehaving.
    Many children will concentrate harder if they know that something "fun" is planned as a reward. But be

careful not to use fun as an ultimate weapon of control. If enjoyment and pleasure are wielded like a club to make students behave, tension and rebellion will only increase. Taking away the most enjoyable moments of the learning process because the students are "bad" or "misbehaving" doesn't take into account the research that shows children learn better when they are enjoying themselves.

What's needed is a balance of both energizing and relaxing techniques. If you talk to students about the value of stimulating their bodies and brains in positive ways, and relaxing to increase learning and retention, they'll have less of a tendency to use the playful moments to go wild. So after a difficult test or a period of great concentration, you might want to plan a light, playful moment to maintain the balance between work and play. If they can see the value of balancing work and play when they are young, it's more likely that their lives as adults will be balanced.

As you begin to use these ideas, start with the activities that seem mild to you. Gradually, you can add more playful elements. Many children today have forgotten how to play cooperatively. One-upmanship will become the rule, not the exception, unless we begin to model and encourage playful, lighthearted self-expression.

Letter 2

Dear Ms. Laffers,
I don't consider myself a funny person, and neither does anyone else. What if I try to do something funny and it doesn't work? I would surely die of embarrassment.

Signed, Grumpy in Gainesville

Ann Replies

Dear Grumpy,
Just as playing in the major leagues is not a prerequisite for throwing and catching a ball, you don't have to be a comedienne in order to use humor and playfulness effectively. But like any skill, the more you practice, the more likely you are to hit a home run.

There are two cardinal rules before you begin to experiment using humor:

1. Take yourself lightly.
2. Realize that your style of humor is unique.

Comparing yourself with other "funny" people can easily lead to denial and disavowal of your particular contribution to humor.

Remember, humor in the classroom is a participatory event, not a comedy show. Great teachers have the ability to model positive playful behavior and support the playfulness of their students. Most humorous moments tend to be situational, not preplanned. So if you can develop an ability to be flexible, spontaneous, and open to what happens in the moment, you'll see new ways of becoming more playful.

As far as dying of embarrassment, what happens when you drop the ball when you're playing catch? Do you automatically throw down your glove, rant and rave about how clumsy and stupid you are, and then stop playing baseball forever? Of course not. You pick up the ball, mutter, "Oops," and concentrate even harder on catching it the next time.

Looking back, my life seems like one long obstacle race, with me its chief obstacle.
– Jack Parr

Treat your momentary "bombs" in the same fashion. Say, "Oops," or shrug your shoulders and move on, knowing it was no great tragedy. If you bomb more than once, remind yourself that very few professional baseball players bat 1000. Using humor is a process of exploration, not an end goal. Your focus shouldn't be trying to make your students laugh, but rather creating a safe environment so that students can risk without criticism or humiliation. If you can laugh at your mistakes, it will give them permission to laugh at their own.

If you become embarrassed and your face turns red, don't deny what has happened. It's an honest reaction. All you need to say is, "I sure am embarrassed," and you'll probably win the hearts of each one of your students. Everyone has been in a similar situation, undoubtedly more than once.

Laughter is the art of making molehills out of mountains.

Letter 3

Dear Ann,
     Even if I have the most brilliant game plan, projects, and ideas, what do I do if my students won't cooperate, risk, or try new things?
     Yours truly, Stuck With Stiff Students

Ann Replies

Dear Stuck,

Of course your students are stiff. They probably haven't been given the permission to play since they left the second grade. The rules of conduct for the classroom are very old, and old patterns don't fade easily. Many students have been led to think, "If I'm having so much fun, I can't possibly be learning anything!" Unfortunately, this mind-set has prevented humor from being integrated into the curriculum and utilized as a communication tool.

As children mature, what strikes them as funny, witty, or playful changes. If you have a group that has adopted the attitude "Nothing's funny," it's a sure bet that they are out of practice. Despite appearances, don't buy into their perspective. A sense of humor never "goes away"; it just changes forms. Perhaps their humor has been turned inside out and upside down, and twisted until it is unrecognizable. It may take some energy to open it again, but it will be well worth the effort.

A belly laugh may be the one true cry of humanity. — Brian Swimme

Don't expect to bring a lethargic, negative group to a state of uproarious laughter within a few weeks! Negativity ("This is stupid . . ."), the feeling of superiority ("I'm too cool to laugh . . ."), and criticism ("You don't know what's happening, man . . .") can all be countered with laughter and humor, but not at once.

One of the first steps you can take is to appeal to students who are still able to smile. Because laughter is infectious, it takes only a few students to see the humor in a situation, and soon more will join them. The most challenging students are the students who have been hurt and humiliated, and who have, for all purposes, given up. If students have low self-esteem, nothing will strike them as humorous. These are the students to focus on. If you can get these students to smile, *even once,* you have opened a door that may not have been opened for a long time. Realize that once a door has been opened, there is an opportunity to open it further.

You can also solicit help from a student who has a natural sense of leadership and play. If the rest of the students see that they have a choice between tenseness and a lighter way, they'll eventually begin to choose the one that brings them more joy.

Letter 4

Dear Ann,

    I used to be a fun-loving, inspired, and highly motivated teacher. Lately, I've been feeling exhausted and overworked. This is partly due to the fact that I can't seem to make any significant changes within the system. I just don't have any energy left to play, smile, or do anything but the barest minimum.

Signed, Paradise Lost

Ann Replies

Dear Paradise Lost,

    Have hope. Paradise may be lost, but it's not forgotten. You seem to be exhibiting the classic symptoms of teacher *burnout,* which is reflected in the dissatisfaction and disillusionment you feel about your job. Social, psychological, and physical factors come into play to produce burnout, so you need to look at all areas of your life to see if you can find the underlying causes. Are you becoming distant from your students and family? Are you feeling as if you are "not quite yourself"? Are you experiencing chronic exhaustion, irritability, depression, sleep disturbances, memory lapses, inability to feel joy, or lack of purpose? These symptoms indicate that your energy is being drained faster than it is being replenished.

    Right now your immune system is very fragile because you have been pushing it past its ability to recover and recuperate. One of the first things to disappear when you are under a great deal of stress is your sense of humor. Your body is giving you a warning signal that shouldn't be trivialized or ignored because 90 percent of most diseases are stress related.

    You must look at both long-term and short-term solutions. Several short-term solutions include the following:

1. Take a short break to reassess your life, before your body forces you to take a long, unexpected one.
2. Find a social support system where you can express rather than suppress your feelings.
3. Engage in some form of mild exercise.
4. Find a "laughing buddy" who can help you see the silver lining inside your personal thundercloud.

194

The most important long-term solution is for you to get outside assistance to help you increase your positive coping mechanisms and balance your work and personal life.

If you're burning out, you may tend to shut down and shut out as much stimulus as you can. If you attempt to shut out the bad, be careful that you don't also shut out the good. Let the joy that others have infuse you. It's perfectly all right to get a happiness transfusion when you need it. Teaching is a process of giving and receiving. Don't ignore your need to have your cup replenished.

Letter 5

Dear Ann,

I am already considered "off the wall" by many of my colleagues and even some of my students. Sometimes I feel I'm all alone in my quest to "lighten" things up at school. If I add any more fuel to the fire, I'm afraid that I might get fired.

Call me, Taut Between a
Rock and a Hard Place

Ann Replies

Dear Taut,

It's great to hear that you still have the ability to be spontaneous and playful, despite the overwhelming odds. Keep up the good work! You're already ten steps ahead of the game. Perhaps you could give laughter lessons to your faculty! Actually, you bring up the serious problem of knowing how to handle peer pressure among your colleagues and staff. It's crucial that you balance your use of humor with your seriousness; otherwise, you may alienate others with your openness to play. This can result in being labeled "weird" or, worse, "unprofessional." And just like any self-adhesive label, once a label has been applied, it's very difficult to remove.

The first thing to do is take a quick pen and paper assessment of your staff and rate them on a humor scale from one to ten. Don't forget to include yourself in this exercise. Rank them from first to last, and see who is closest to you on the scale. Then make sure to burn the list! This is not an exercise in blame and condemnation, but in looking realistically at an important personality trait. It sounds as if you might be at the top of the list, which can be good and bad. What you need to do is increase the advantages and decrease any disadvantages.

After you have rated your staff, see who's at the bottom of the list. If you use this person as your gauge to see if you are "acting appropriately," you'll probably lose any positive qualities that you've developed because that person will frown upon any activity that has a spark of life in it. Because any group only moves as quickly as its slowest member, this may be the person who's holding the group back. But don't despair – change is always possible.

Pay attention to the people who are in the middle of the list. They are the best indicators whether your behavior is inappropriate for the situation. If you sense that you are alienating them, back off a bit and try to gently engage them in your playfulness to discover how they play. This will encourage, not discourage, the kind of behavior you are trying to elicit. Practice this technique by slowly working your way down the list until you can relate playfully to the last person on your list. By then, you might be surprised to find that you see that person differently. Remember, it's up to you to build the kind of world that you want to live in.

Letter 6

Dear Ann,
My principal is very conservative. What if she disapproves of using laughter in the classroom and won't support the idea?
Sincerely, Confused
About Principals
and Principles

Ann Replies

Dear Confused,
Because more and more students appear to lack self-control, many teachers feel successful if they've kept control in their classrooms during the day. Lately, the focus

has shifted from educating students to containing, maintaining, and sustaining order. Unfortunately, laughter in the classroom is often equated with chaos in the classroom. This is a myth that needs to be dispelled, because laughter is a softening influence and promotes learning.

When students feel at ease, secure, and happy, they are less likely to act out, harm others, or be destructive. Confidence stems from the ability to master oneself, and mastery is obtained through self-knowledge. Part of education's role is to help students to know themselves. Although all students have their hidden agendas, they also share several basic human needs. They need to understand and fit into the world around them. If we can show students how to use laughter instead of violence to overcome obstacles, we have given a great gift to the world.

Another objective of education is to help students to become expansive and precise in their thinking. Clarity of thought cannot happen when fear is present, because fear and joy cannot coexist. But there's good news: Fear disappears in the presence of laughter. Too often, curiosity and eagerness are destroyed because of an excessive use of threat, ridicule, or punishment to keep control.

Students who cannot or will not laugh may be angry, depressed, or in conflict. Your principal needs to see that laughter is a strong indication that healing is taking place. Laughter is more than mere silliness or fun. At the deepest level, it's the recognition that pain can be overcome. Thus, you are not only helping the students to learn more easily, you are also modeling a valuable life skill.

If running a tight ship is a priority for your principal, then you must find a creative way to show her that humor can be the glue that bonds each element of the ship together so that it stays afloat. Don't forget that your principal is also under a great deal of pressure. Try the softening influence of levity with your principal, even if she seems totally devoid of humor. A smile a day may be all that it takes to banish the *grim* reaper.

Letter 7

Dear Ann Laffers,

I hardly have enough time to get through the mandated curriculum as it is. How can I find the time to add in something that feels as if it's extraneous?

Sincerely, On the Brink

Ann Replies

Dear On the Brink,

Granted, there is hardly enough time to do all that is required of you as a teacher, but moments of spontaneous laughter integrated into your day will probably take less time than speaking a cross or harsh word admonishing your students to pay attention. Attention cannot be forced, as you well know. The element of surprise will always get a student's attention. Human beings enjoy the unexpected if it's positive in nature. Many times we laugh because we are surprised.

If you feel that adding humor is just another element that will throw you off track, or that it is competing with those things that absolutely must be done, you might find yourself consistently putting off playful moments until all of the required work is done. New teachers often feel as though they don't have enough activities to fill the day. Experienced teachers never have enough days to finish their activities! Because there is a never-ending supply of work that needs to be accomplished, it's easy to put aside something new or unfamiliar until later. Unfortunately, later never arrives.

If you are experimenting with a new technique, it will take time to become comfortable with it. Trial and error takes more time than using a familiar technique. The objective is to make humor an integral part of your day rather than using it only after completing serious work.

If you still find it too difficult to justify taking the time to experiment with new techniques, remember that humor isn't always activity oriented. Humor arises out of the moment. The key for increasing your capacity to experience joy is the willingness to be open to delight. Delightful moments abound if we take the time to see them.

Healthy human beings will always choose pleasure over pain, and they will do everything in their power to find it. Students are no exception. If they are participating in a negative game, such as "Let's see who can break the pencil first," no doubt their pleasure comes from the element of surprise, a feeling of superiority or accomplishment. If you take away their pencils, they will find another game to play. The key is to bring a sufficient amount of pleasure and surprise into the learning curriculum, so that students can learn to direct their playfulness in a positive direction.

Letter 8

Ann Replies

Dear All Work,

Most adults want respect simply because they are adults. They figure that they deserve it based solely on the fact that they survived their childhood and adolescence. Demanding respect that has not been earned is nothing more than a power play. This kind of play is the most harmful to the creative spirit and to the love for learning. This attitude becomes more predominant at the university level. Some professors derive pleasure from creating undue stress for their students simply because they had to endure a difficult passage to earn their position of power. This becomes a self-perpetuating "do unto them" cycle.

To be credible means that you are believable and trustworthy. If you are inconsistent or if you exhibit a double standard with students, you will lose credibility. Students can sense deception. If you are a person who says, "Do as I say and not as I do," then you are giving your students permission to follow suit.

Today, educators have many shoes to fill. They have to be part social worker, part alcohol and drug specialist, part spiritual mentor, part role model, and part surrogate parent. It's a wonder that any factual knowledge is imparted. It is crucial, now more than ever, that students feel a deep sense of confidence in you, because your role has become that of a guide. Your students need assistance to learn how to "do" and how to "be."

So what happens if you add the spice of humor to your interactions with your students? Will you become more or less trustworthy? It's difficult to trust someone you don't like, no matter how knowledgeable that person is. And if you are liked,

199

you will undoubtedly gain your students' admiration and respect. Do not, however, become a prankster. Pranksters get their laughs at the expense of others. If you can model a passion for learning and a wide knowledge base while showing your students that you enjoy teaching, they'll learn that they can look forward to becoming adults.

Some believe that the only thing education has in common with entertainment is the letter "e." We must be careful not to categorize all entertainment as a passive diversion. It's possible to be thoroughly entertained by participating in an event or project, even if it's one that requires effort. Learning should be engaging, more than entertaining. The brain loves to learn and will become dull unless it is given stimulus. If you are operating on "automatic pilot," your students will know it, and you will lose your credibility and the respect of your students. But if you have enthusiasm for your subject matter and convey it in creative and playful ways, you will surely evoke the deepest level of respect from your students—that of awe.

Letter 9

Dear Ms. Laffers,

Get real, Ann! I am a high school math teacher and football coach. These techniques may work well for younger students, but you'll have to convince me that they'll work with my classes.

Sign me, Skeptical

Ann Replies

Dear Skeptical,

Henry Ford once said, "Whether you think you can or think you can't, you are right." The only way that you'll be convinced of the value of utilizing laughter in the classroom or a lighthearted teaching touch will be to experience the results for yourself. No amount of information or stories that I could share with you will change your mind if your mind is already made up. Ask yourself, "Am I willing to try?" If you feel that the effort is not worth your time, then you might want to heed the advice of Professor Oops, who says, "Don't just do something; sit there!" Most halfhearted attempts end in failure and are justified with the smug comment "I told you so!" In reality, the effort was doomed to fail because it's impossible to start a car with a dead battery.

If you are willing to adopt the motto of one of the astronauts, which was, "Not a day without discovery," and if you are willing to accept a jump-start to turn your engine, then you are on your way to true adventures in learning.

Another question to ask yourself is, what is my coaching style? Your style of coaching may be a reflection of your teaching/humor style. As a coach, you play many roles for your athletes. You make demands, offer support and encouragement, set goals, and give praise when goals are reached. The ultimate goal of any great coach is to help athletes to develop their own internal coach so that their motivation doesn't leave when you do. Be aware that if your style is to berate or negate students, some transference will occur, and a negative self-concept may be internalized. That's the danger of strong-arm coaching. You could be unconsciously programming your young athletes to see themselves as failures because they can't reach a time-specific goal.

This harmful self-talk appears later in life. Many corporations have spent money on humor and self-esteem seminars to help their employees shift away from the highly competitive and self-negating attitudes adopted from earlier influences.

As a coach, you have the power to show your students a positive way of handling difficult problems and an opportunity to model a new level of performance. But if your humor is filled with put-downs and negative remarks, you are defeating yourself in the long run. Albert Schweitzer said, "Example is not the main thing in influencing others. It is the only thing."

So, there you have it: Set yourself a positive humor goal, Coach. Challenge yourself to reach it, and enjoy yourself and your team in the process!

Letter 10

Dear Ann,
    I have a student who thinks everything is funny. I can't get him to settle down and concentrate. He makes a joke of everything. I'm at a loss about what do with him. Can you help?
            Signed, Not a Joking Matter

Ann Replies

Dear No Joke,

You do, indeed, have a challenging situation on your hands, because your student has developed habits that are working against both of you. Laughing and "seeing everything as a joke" are two different viewpoints, and so it's important to discover the root cause of your student's attitude. Ask yourself the following questions: Is he using humor to procrastinate? Is he spontaneously funny? Is he reacting or interacting? Does he use the moment to gain attention, or does he exhibit bizarre behavior unrelated to anything external? If you sense that there isn't a physical or emotional cause for his behavior (such as alcohol or drug abuse, or escape from emotional trauma), then you may simply have a class clown on your hands.

No doubt your class clown's humor is disrupting the other students around him and causing you to spend more time dealing with his behavior than you'd like. If this is the case, you might want to give him positive strokes and nonverbal reinforcement (eye contact or smiling) when you catch him "doing something right," because his objective is to get your attention. Keep the wise words of Goethe in mind: "Correction does much, but encouragement does more." The challenge for you will be to refrain from countering his thrusts and parries with your own.

If he is a natural comic, it may be useful for you to find healthy outlets for his humor, so that it doesn't seep out sideways and catch you off guard. He's probably getting a lot of reinforcement from his peers for his joking, in which case you could dubb him "Official Friday Joke Teller or Storyteller" or create another role for him to express his talents.

The most important step is to communicate directly with your "jokester," acknowledge his talent, but clearly explain the classroom rules and the consequences of breaking them. See if you can come to a mutual agreement about the appropriate use of his humor. If you can appreciate, or even laugh at his humor, there's a good chance that he'll respect your needs as well.

202

42

Glossary and "Giggliography"

Glossary of Terms

Attention Deficit: A skill developed to survive the morning announcements.

Binomial: What happens when you don't like what's being served in the cafeteria.

Bulletin Board: What is retrieved by the Kindergarten Cop.

Cafeteria: A real mess hall.

Computerize: What you get when you stare at a video display terminal for more than twenty minutes.

Concrete Learning: Mix mastery.

Cooperative Learning: A prerequisite for cooperative buying.

Dysfunctional: A syndrome that happens when the *fun* is removed and the *funk* takes over.

Early Retirement: What teachers do at 9:00 P.M. after a tiring day.

Eraseophobia: Fear of chalk dust.

Fluorescent Lighting: The kind of lighting that takes the brain waves on a "fluo-ride."

Fund-raiser: Used as an excuse to bake cookies; raises funds and cholesterol levels.

Hall Monitors: Low-tech surveillance systems.

Hall Passes: Sanctioned bladder controls.

Homework: Household chores you tackle on the "weak-ends."

Inoculate: The shot you decide to get *after* you've been infected.

In-service: The opposite of out-of-service.

Intercom System: The opposite of a nervous system.

IQ: A Japanese form of poetry.

Kinesthetic Learning: Relatives who take night courses in art appreciation.

Lesson Plans: Formal outlines written two weeks after the lesson has been taught.

Map: What most teachers would like to take at around one o'clock in the afternoon.

M Teams: An educational concept that began in Kansas with Auntie Em.

Multiple Intelligences: Mental traits that have evolved to cope with multiple-choice tests.

Paradox: Who you'll wind up seeing if you don't take care of yourself.

Parent-Teacher Conferences: A feat of scheduling; a covert test for multiple intelligence.

Paycheck: Something often spent two weeks before receiving it.

Pension Plan: A phenomenon often known to bring on pension headaches.

Perpetual Vacation Machine: Yet to be invented.

Professional Days: The stupor that results after attempting to implement all the required changes.

Reading Readiness: When you finally heed the Surgeon General's warning.

Sick Leave: What you accrue if you don't catch the flu.

Site-based Management: The opposite of blindly based management.

Staff Meetings: The time you're allotted to do your lesson plans.

Sub: The sandwich you can eat half of within a twenty-minute lunch period.

Teachers' Convention: A great time to go shopping.

Teachers' Lounge: A storeroom for ashtrays, treats, old magazines, and notices for pyramid distributorships.

The Gifted: Those who announce the date of their birth.

Time on Task: Inversely proportional to the amount of planning time you're allotted to prepare for the task.

Time-out: Lunch with your staff at a local restaurant.

TLC: An acronym for "The Laughing Classroom."

Volunteer Committees: Something you're required to chair at least one of.

Window of Opportunity: Something you're allowed to open only after you've washed it.

"Giggliography"

We highly recommend the following list of books for your personal library. They will aid you with your professional growth and insure that you remain on the cutting edge of your field. There is, however, one small requirement. If you want them, you'll have to write them!

Blanche, Tom. *Teaching Twitches and Learning Itches.* Chicago: Panic Press, 1987.

Brain, Brian. *Teach and Grow Weary.* New York: Sorrow & Sorrow & Sons, 1958.

Cain, Abel. *The Hallway Less Traveled.* Garden City Park, NY: Bowling Alley Press, 1989.

Campbell, Soupy. *The Cafeteria Food Digest.* London, England: Intestine Press, 1976.

Chopp, Woody. *The Martial Art of Teaching.* New York: Buckle-Down Publishing Co., 1991.

Cycle, Don, M.D., III. *Seasonal Affect Bulletin Board Disorder.* San Diego, CA: Brace Yourself, Inc., 1987.

Dune, Sandy. *Overcoming Ninja-itus.* New York: Row, Row & Row, Inc., 1991.

Fulcrum, Bobby. *Everything I Ever Wanted to Know I Learned Incorrectly.* Washington, DC: Wrong & Sons, 1990.

Guy, Guy. *Looking Out for Numbers One, Two, and Three.* Tacoma, WA: Meenie, Mienie, Mo Press, 1987.

Hardwood, Sparrow. *Teachers Who Collect Too Much*. New York: Doubleup and Co., 1989.

Mo, Dot. *The Incomplete Guide to Giving Incompletes*. New York: Wed Wooster Books, 1988.

Pill, Bill. *Multidisciplinary Vitamins and Teacher Supplements*. Orange, CA: Swallow Press, Inc., 1991.

Rapper, Eric. *Career Opportunities That Knock Twice*. Santa Fe, NM: Nevermore & Sons, 1954.

Smyth, Wesson. *The One-Minute Hall Monitor*. San Francisco: Lone Wolf Press, 1990.

Swamped, Sherri. *How to Substitute for Substitutes*. Lansing, MI: Tried & True Publishers, 1980.

Tailor, Wiley. *Classroom Conundrums and Other Rhythm Instruments*. Chicago: Bongo & Co., 1977.

Tell, Bill. *Thriving on Chaos in the Classroom*. Andromeda, CA: Nebula Publishers, 2012.

Thum, Thomas. *Questions Not to Ask Your Principal*. New York: Frown Publishers, 1989.

Whinot, Tammi. *1001 Creative Ways to Use Chalk*. Santa Fe, NM: Fingernail Press, 1984.

Xeroxx, Lillith. *How to Copy Copyrighted Material*. New York: Carbon Copies Press, 1998.

Yin, Yang. *Zen and the Art of Lesson Planning*. Princeton, NJ: Mantra Publishers, 1990.

Zorro, Brutus. *The Joys of Tag-Team Teaching*. New York: Golden Glove Publishers, 1988.

43

Lighten Up Your Lounge!

1. Bring joke books, humorous magazines, or other funny reading material.
2. Make a quick-snooze corner; have a small tape recorder with relaxation tapes, earphones, and a pillow available.
3. Place fresh-cut or dried flowers—everywhere.
4. Feeling too "a-dull-tified"? Make a bulletin board and have the teachers bring in pictures of themselves at the same ages as the students they currently teach.
5. Create a doodle corner. Supply markers, paper, and unusual items to color, such as copies of an 8×10 picture of the staff.
6. If you have a refrigerator in the room, place an unusual food or gag item inside it to surprise the staff.
7. Bring in your favorite windup toys or a large stuffed toy mascot.
8. Photocopy funny or uplifting stories, and leave extra copies for others to have.
9. Donate something fun to the lounge—giant blowup crayons, plants, pictures, lamps, rugs, or fun chairs, such as a rocking chair, lazy boy, or hammock.
10. Keep a large blank art book in the lounge, and encourage everyone to write jokes, stories, or quotations in it.
11. Create a "tacky table" where you display "white-elephant" items you consider tacky.
12. Don't wait for the holiday parties. Plan a social event or two during slow times.
13. Occasionally put something unexpected in the room, such as balloons or a bowl of fortune cookies.
14. Once a month, have a potluck lunch together. Even if you're on different schedules, bring enough for everyone to share.
15. Every day, give a compliment to at least three teachers.
16. Once a month, hire a professional masseuse to give five-minute shoulder massages to all who want them.
17. Take walks together. Put up a sign-up sheet.
18. Donate stress thermometers, and place them in a jar for teachers to use when they want to check their stress level.
19. Declare one day a week "Noncomplaint Day." Anyone who complains gets docked ten cents.
20. Choose a teacher of the week or month. Give that teacher fun gifts that cost a dollar or less.

All of the animals excepting man know that the principal business of life is to enjoy it.
—Samuel Butler

44

Classroom Checklist

We have compiled this list of inexpensive items that will transform your classroom into a safe and happy environment where playfulness and humor can flourish. Many of the items below have been gathered from the Warm-ups, Play Breaks, Laughing Lessons, and the Fast and Fun: Thirty Ideas sections.

- ☐ Area Rugs
- ☐ Art Supplies
    - ☐ Crayons
    - ☐ Magic Markers
    - ☐ Paints
    - ☐ Paper
- ☐ Balloons
- ☐ Balls
    - ☐ Rubber
    - ☐ Sponge
    - ☐ Stuffed Planet
- ☐ Bean Bags
- ☐ Bells 
- ☐ Boxes
    - ☐ "Daffy-nitions" Box
    - ☐ Longest Word Box
    - ☐ Praise-the-Teacher Box
    - ☐ Suggestions Box
    - ☐ Surprise Box
    - ☐ Unusual Word Box
- ☐ Bright Colors
- ☐ Bulletin Boards
    - ☐ Baby Picture Board
    - ☐ Great Quotes Board
    - ☐ Positive Graffiti
    - ☐ Student of the Week

- ☐ Camera
- ☐ Cassette Player and Headphones
- ☐ Colored Chalk
- ☐ Costume Pieces
- ☐ Flags and Banners
- ☐ Flowers
- ☐ Hammock
- ☐ Hanging Chair
- ☐ Hats
    - ☐ Announcements Hat
    - ☐ Assignments Hat
    - ☐ Joke Brown Bag for Over the Head
    - ☐ Reminder Hat
    - ☐ You're Terrific Hat
- ☐ Lamps
- ☐ Laughter Tape
- ☐ Live Animals
    - ☐ Aquarium
    - ☐ Terrarium
- ☐ Masks
    - ☐ Cultural
    - ☐ Handmade
- ☐ Mobiles
- ☐ Musical Instruments
    - ☐ Drums
    - ☐ Gong
    - ☐ Noisemakers
    - ☐ Whistles

- ☐ Music Tapes
  - ☐ Classical
  - ☐ Energetic
  - ☐ Environmental
  - ☐ Relaxing
- ☐ Noses
  - ☐ Animal
  - ☐ Banana
  - ☐ Clown
  - ☐ Groucho Marx
- ☐ Photographs
- ☐ Pillows
- ☐ Plants
- ☐ Posters
  - ☐ Affirmations
  - ☐ Humorous
  - ☐ Inspiring
  - ☐ Outdoor scenes

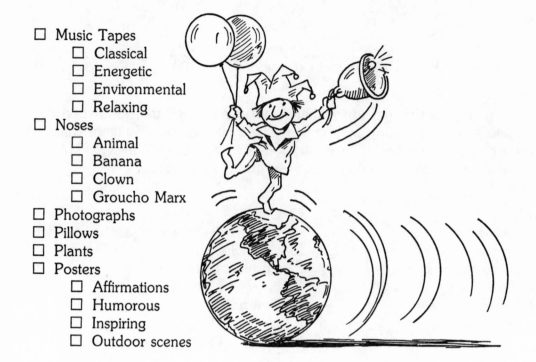

45

Song: "The Rattle Hymn"

This song is sung to the tune of "The Battle Hymn of the Republic."

Mine eyes have seen how humor
Strikes a universal chord.
It's now tumbling out of classrooms
Causing minds to be restored.
It has loosed the fateful, frightening plight
Of students who are bored.
Laughter is catching on.

Glory, glory, humor to ya,
Glory, glory, humor to ya,
Glory, glory, humor to ya,
Laughter is catching on.

The beauty of all laughter is
It's joy that we can see.
In the story told by students,
They are learning happily.
If you take the time to laugh and smile,
No doubt you will agree – that
Laughter is catching on.

Glory, glory, humor to ya,
Glory, glory, humor to ya,
Glory, glory, humor to ya,
Laughter is catching on.

46

Humor Homework

1. Buy a blank notebook. Paste cartoons that make you laugh on the cover. Write any funny moments you notice during school in your notebook.

2. Create your own laughter rules for your teachers' lounge.

3. Use the classroom checklist to begin adding humorous elements to your teaching environment. Get creative input from your students.

4. Write a question you have about humor to Ann Laffers, and have your students answer it as though they were Ann. Then post their responses.

5. Create a funny bumper sticker or slogan for your school or class.

47

Play Sheet

1. What causes you the most stress during your teaching day? List several techniques you could use to see this from a more humorous perspective.

2. Recall a time when you were hurt through the use of humor. Write how this affected you.

3. Read one book from the bibliography, and list three fun ideas that you can apply during your teaching day.

4. Imagine your ideal laughing classroom. What are the elements in your classroom, your students, and your teaching style that make it a success?

5. Divide a sheet of paper in half. On one side, list every reason you can't/shouldn't/ won't use laughter more often as a communication tool in your classroom. On the other side, list why it's important to have a laughing classroom.

48
Notes for Myself

Bibliography

Activities

Christopher, Milbourne. *Milbourne Christopher's Magic Book*. New York: Harper & Row, 1977.

Cohen, Kenneth K. *Imagine That! A Child's Guide to Yoga*. Santa Barbara, CA: Santa Barbara Press, 1983.

Darrow, Helen Fisher. *Independent Activities for Creative Learning*. New York: Columbia University Teachers College Press, 1986.

Drew, Naomi. *Learning the Skills of Peacemaking*. Rolling Hills Estates, CA: Jalmar Press, 1989.

Faverty, Richard. *Bubble Handbook*. Schenevus, NY: Greenleaf Publishers, 1987.

Goelitz, Jeffrey. *The Ultimate Kid: Levels of Learning That Make a Difference*. Boulder Creek, CA: Planetary Publications, 1986.

Hirsch, E. D., Jr. *A First Dictionary of Cultural Literacy: What Our Children Need to Know*. Boston: Houghton Mifflin, 1989.

Kincher, Jonni. *Dreams Can Help*. Minneapolis: Free Spirit Press, 1990.

McCutcheon, Randall. *Get Off My Brain*. Minneapolis: Free Spirit Press, 1990.

_____. *Can You Find It?* Rev. ed. Minneapolis: Free Spirit Press, 1991.

Newman, Frederick R. *MouthSounds*. New York: Workman Publishing, 1980.

Simon, Sarina. *101 Amusing Ways to Develop Your Child's Thinking Skills and Creativity*. Los Angeles: RGA Publications, 1989.

Striker, Susan. *Build a Better Mousetrap: An Anti-Coloring Book*. New York: Holt, Rinehart and Winston, 1983.

Vaughan, Alan. *Incredible Coincidence*. New York: Ballantine Books, 1979.

Wills, Russel, and Hendricks, Gay. *Awareness Activities for Children*. Englewood Cliffs, NJ: Prentice-Hall, 1975.

Creativity

Bagley, Michael T., and Hess, Karin. *Two Thousand Ways of Using Imagery in the Classroom*. New York: Trillium Press, 1984.

Barrett, Susan L. *It's All in Your Head: A Guide to Understanding Your Brain and Boosting Your Brain Power*. Minneapolis: Free Spirit Press, 1985.

Caney, Steven. *Steven Caney's Invention Book*. New York: Workman Publishing, 1985.

Carr, Rachel. *Be a Frog, Be a Bird, Be a Tree*. New York: Harper & Row, 1977.

DeBono, Edward. *Lateral Thinking*. New York: Harper & Row, 1970.

DeMille, Richard. *Put Your Mother on the Ceiling*. New York: Penguin Books, 1976.

Gilbert, Anne. *Teaching the Three R's Through Movement*. Minneapolis: Burgess Publishing, 1977.

McKisson, Micki. *Chrysalis: Nurturing Creative and Independent Thought in Children*. Tucson, AZ: Zephyr Press, AZ, 1984.

Perkins, David. *The Mind's Best Work: A New Psychology of Creative Thinking*. Cambridge, MA: Harvard University Press, 1983.

Rico, Gabriel. *Writing the Natural Way*. Los Angeles: J. P. Tarcher, 1983.

Shallcross, Doris. *Teaching Creative Behavior*. Englewood Cliffs, NJ: Prentice-Hall, 1981.

Sternberg, R. *Beyond I.Q.: A Triarchic Theory of Human Intelligence*. New York: Cambridge University Press, 1984.

Vitale, Barbara Meister. *Unicorns Are Real: A Right-Brained Approach to Learning*. Tucson, AZ: Zephyr Press, AZ, 1982.

Williams, Linda. *Teaching for the Two-Sided Mind*. Englewood Cliffs, NJ: Prentice-Hall, 1983.

Games

Caney, Steven. *Steven Caney's Play Book*. New York: Workman Publishing, 1975.

Cassidy, John. *Juggling for the Complete Klutz*. Palo Alto, CA: Klutz Press, 1990.

Fisher, Richard. *Brain Games*. New York: Schocken Books, 1982.

Fluegelman, Andrew, ed. *The New Games Book*. San Francisco: Headlands Press, 1976.

Grunfeld, Frederic V., ed. *Games of the World: How to Make Them, How to Play Them, How They Came to Be*. New York: Holt, Rinehart and Winston, 1975.

Juggletime Instructional Video. Edmonds, WA: Jugglebug, 1991.

Orlick, Terry. *The Cooperative Sports and Games Books*. New York: Pantheon, 1978.

_____. *The Second Cooperative Sports and Games Book*. New York: Pantheon, 1982.

Rice, Rydberg, and Yaconelli. *Fun N Games*. Grand Rapids, MI: Zondervan, 1977.

Rohnke, Karl. *Silver Bullets: A Guide to Initiative Problems, Adventure Games and Trust Activities*. Dubuque, IA: Kendall Hunt, 1989.

Weinstein, Matt, and Goodman, Joel. *Playfair: Everybody's Guide to Noncompetitive Play*. San Luis Obispo, CA: Impact Publishers, 1980.

Humor

Adams, Joey. *Encyclopedia of Humor* New York: Bonanza Books, 1968.

Allen, Steve. *Funny People*. New York: Stein and Day, 1981.

_____. *More Funny People*. New York: Stein and Day, 1982.

_____. *How to Be Funny*. New York: McGraw-Hill, 1987.

Armour, Richard. *A Diabolical Dictionary of Education*. New York: McGraw-Hill, 1969.

Asimov, Isaac. *Treasury of Humor*. Boston: Houghton Mifflin, 1971.

Bloch, Arthur. *Murphy's Law and Other Reasons Why Things Go Wrong*. Los Angeles: Price, Stern, & Sloan Publishers, 1977.

_____. *Murphy's Law, Book Two*. Los Angeles: Price, Stern, & Sloan Publishers, 1980.

Blumenfeld, Ester, and Alpern, Lynne. *The Smile Connection*. Englewood Cliffs, NJ: Prentice-Hall, 1986.

Brody, R. "Anatomy of a Laugh." *American Health*, Nov.–Dec. 1983:41–7.

Cousins, Norman. *Anatomy of an Illness*. New York: Bantam Books, 1979.

_____. *The Healing Heart*. New York: W. W. Norton, 1983.

Eastman, Max. *Enjoyment of Laughter*. New York: Simon & Schuster, 1936.

Frey, William H., II. *Crying: The Mystery of Tears*. Minneapolis: Winston Press, 1985.

Fry, William F., Jr. *Sweet Madness: A Study of Humor*. Palo Alto, CA: Pacific Books, 1963.

Goldstein, Jeffrey H. "A Laugh a Day." *The Sciences*, Vol. 22, 1982, pp. 21–25.

Goldstein, J. H., and McGhee, P. *The Psychology of Humor: Theoretical Perspectives and Empirical Issues*. New York: Academic Press, 1972.

_____ and _____, eds. *Handbook of Humor Research*. New York: Springer-Verlag, 1983.

Klein, Alan. *The Healing Power of Humor*. Los Angeles: J. P. Tarcher, 1989.

Larson, Gary. *The Far Side*. Kansas City, MO: Andrews, McMeel, and Parker, 1982.

Laughing Matters (magazine). Joel Goodman, ed. Available from the Humor Project, Saratoga Institute, 110 Springs St., Saratoga Springs, NY 12866.

Laughter Works (newsletter). Available from 222 Selby Ranch Rd., Suite 4, Sacramento, CA 95864.

Mamchak, P. Susan, and Mamchak, Steven B. *Educator's Lifetime Library of Stories, Quotes, Anecdotes, Wit and Humor*. West Nyack, NY: Parker Publishing Company, 1979.

Mancke, R., et al. "Clowning: A Healing Process." *Health Education*, Oct.–Nov. 1984, 15(6):16.

McGhee, Paul E. *Humor: Origins and Development*. San Francisco: W. H. Freeman, 1979.

Mindess, H. *Laughter and Liberation*. Los Angeles: Nash Publishing, 1971.

_____. *The Antioch Humor Test: Making Sense of Humor*. New York: Argon Books, 1985.

Moody, Raymond A. *Laugh After Laugh*. Jacksonville, FL: Headwaters Press, 1978.

Peter, Laurence J., and Dana, Bill. *The Laughter Prescription*. New York: Ballantine Books, 1982.

Peterson, Norma. *Teachers: A Survival Guide*. New York: New American Library, 1985.

Pyke, Magnus. *Weird and Wonderful Science Facts*. New York: Sterling Publishing, 1984.

Stears, F. R. *Laughing: Physiology, Pathology, Psychology, Pathopsychology and Development*. Springville, IL: Charles C. Thomas, 1972.

Walker, Barbara. *Laughing Together: Giggles and Grins From Around the World*. Minneapolis: Free Spirit Press, 1992.

Weber, Bruce. *The Funniest Moments in School*. New York: M. Evans and Company, 1974.

Whole Mirth Catalog. Available from 1034 Page St., San Francisco, CA 94117.

Magic

Scarne, John. *Scarne's Magic Tricks*. New York: Crown Publishers, 1951.

Parenting

Baldwin, Rahima. *You Are Your Child's First Teacher*. Berkeley, CA: Celestial Arts, 1989.

Berends, Polly. *Whole Child, Whole Parent*. New York: Harper & Row, 1983.

Greene, Lawrence. *1001 Ways to Improve Your Child's Schoolwork*. New York: Dell, 1991.

Jenkins, Peggy. *The Joyful Child: A Sourcebook of Activities and Ideas for Releasing Children's Natural Joy*. Tucson, AZ: Harbinger House, 1989.

Kersey, Katharine. *Sensitive Parenting: From Infancy to Adulthood*. Reston, VA: Acropolis Books, 1983.

Krueger, Caryl Waller. *Working Parent-Happy Child*. Nashville, TN: Abingdon Press, 1990.

Johnson, June. *838 Ways to Amuse a Child*. New York: Gramercy Publishing, 1950.

Mann, Richard. *The Wonderful Father*. Chicago: Turnbull & Willoughby, 1985.

Perry, Susan. *Playing Smart: A Parent's Guide to Enriching, Offbeat Learning Activities for Ages 4–14*. Minneapolis: Free Spirit Press, 1990.

Self-Esteem

Borba, Michele. *Esteem Builders K–8*. Rolling Hills Estates, CA: Jalmar Press, 1989.

Canfield, J., and Wells, H. *One Hundred Ways to Enhance Self-Concept in the Classroom*. Englewood Cliffs, NJ: Prentice-Hall, 1976.

Kaufman, Gershen, and Raphael, Lev. *Stick Up for Yourself! Every Kid's Guide to Personal Power and Positive Self-Esteem*. Minneapolis: Free Spirit Press, 1990.

Kincher, Jonni. *Psychology for Kids: Forty Tests That Help You Learn About Yourself*. Minneapolis: Free Spirit Press, n.d.

Loomans, Diane. *The Lovables in the Kingdom of Self-Esteem*. Tiburon, CA: HJ Kramer/Starseed Press, 1991.

Loomans, D., Kolberg, K., and Loomans, J. *Positively Mother Goose*. Tiburon, CA: HJ Kramer/Starseed Press, 1991.

Wordplay

Dickson, Paul. *Family Words: The Dictionary for People Who Don't Know a Frone From a Brinkle*. Reading, MA: Addison-Wesley, 1988.

Hall, Rich. *Sniglets*. New York: Collier Books, Macmillan, 1984.

_____. *More Sniglets*. New York: Collier Books, Macmillan, 1985.

Kushner, Maureen, and Hoffman, Sanford. *Great All-Time Excuse Book*. New York: Sterling Publishing, 1990.

McMillan, Bruce A. *Punography*. New York: Penguin Books, 1978.

_____. *Punography Too*. New York: Penguin Books, 1980.

Parlett, David. *Over One Hundred of the World's Best Word Games*. New York: Pantheon Books, 1981.

Rheingold, Howard. *They Have a Word for It: A Lightheated Lexicon of Untranslatable Words and Phrases*. Los Angeles: J. P. Tarcher, 1988.

Rosenbloom, Joseph. *The World's Toughest Tongue Twisters*. New York: Sterling Publishing, 1987.

_____. *696 Silly School Jokes & Riddles*. New York: Sterling Publishing, 1987.

Seymour, Elizabeth. *Hobble-de-hoy! The Word Game for Geniuses*. Salisbury, CT: Lime Rock Press, n.d.

"Backword"
"drowkcaB"

By Professor Oops! (aka Sky Schultz, Ph.D.)

It is difficult to be muddleheaded and difficult to be intelligent.
It is even more difficult to graduate from
intelligence to muddleheadedness.
Chen Pan-Ch'ao, Artist-Poet, Ch'ing Dynasty

I think Diane and Karen are fools. But that is okay. I'm a fool, too—a Professional Fool. I come from a long line of professional fools and inventors. For example, my ancestor, Michelangelo Benedetti Rafael Oops! invented the satellite dish, television receiver, and the truck muffler back in A.D. 1217. Unfortunately, like many artists and visionaries, he was a bit ahead of his time (before the invention of electricity and trucks). But he was a visionary fool—a bit like Karen and Diane. It seems to me that we need the Professional Fool these days with all the amateurs running around. But since I am an expert on "foolosophy," perhaps I should explain what I mean in more detail.

In the Native American tradition, for example, there were people who were designated (or self-appointed) as the "official fools." Sometimes they were known as "contraries—those who did things backward." They walked backward, rode their horses backward, danced backward; in fact, everything they did was contrary to the established norms. These were folks who "did things differently," shook people up, and changed their thinking. Their role was to keep their people from getting stuck in rigid ways of thinking and living. And the fool, in many other times and cultures, was a very important and even sacred role.

The fool never seems to get things "quite right"; that is, he/she never seems to see things the same way as the general culture. Fools provide, however, not only

218

comic relief, but often a more cosmic and timeless perspective that is often missing from those caught up in the practicalities of everyday life. Fools help remind us of what our original goals were, before we got caught up in the day-to-day struggles of "fixing things," making compromises, and surviving.

Diane and Karen remind us what education was originally about: the joy of learning and exploring the unknown with a sense of adventure. And if you knew them as I do, you would know that they live what they teach. They have learned that real education can't be "given" to others, that learning must be "grasped." They know that a person who is mightily motivated to learn will learn under almost any situation—and that a teacher's main job is to help people fall in love with learning.

Diane and Karen demonstrate this by who they are as persons. They show that it is tremendous fun to use every shred of your potential for worthwhile projects, and they believe that learning, loving, and living are as natural and spontaneous as breathing. Of course, all children instinctively know this. Unfortunately, many adults have been damaged and have been taught to be afraid of zestful, learning-full living. But didn't that holy fool, Christ, say something about "Unless ye become as little children, ye shall not enter the kingdom of heaven"? I think he was talking about the kingdom of joy, fulfillment, and happiness. But maybe that's just my foolish opinion.

Diane and Karen are "contraries" of a sort. They help us go backward, back to the natural child within us, back to the child who still loves to learn and laugh. Laughter's essence is surprise, and the essence of wonder and learning is also surprise. This is the joy of the new, the unexpected, and the unknown. We naturally are the most curious creatures, more so than cats or monkeys. The spark of curiosity and wonder is *so* precious. Albert Einstein said, "I have no special gift, I am only passionately curious." If this spark is not extinguished, learning simply "happens."

Teachers need to nourish the spark, but to do that, they need to be keepers of the "flame" themselves. If we are alive to the joy of learning, we may well infect those who have temporarily lost this joyful affliction—and the metaphor is sometimes apt, for learning comes hidden in the disguise of pain, confusion, and doubt. These are really learning's friends too. Diane and Karen have learned to embrace all of learning's friends to explore the many rooms that constitute the mansion of the mind. To be an explorer who attempts to open all levels of human consciousness requires a bit of foolishness and madness. But as Katzantzakis' fool, Zorba, said, "One needs a bit of madness to cut the rope and be free." And don't feel you have to be an expert on "foolosophy" to regain some of your own childlike foolishness. You don't have to be an expert, for amateur fools are "wonder-fool," too. Beware, however; you may get hooked and fall in love with that little playful child within you that loves to "fool around." You might find yourself so full of joy you'll never return to the "*adullt*" you once were. Max Wertheimer said, "An adult is just a deteriorated child."

To begin to be our own fool, simply listen to your unique brand of madness.

B.U. is my motto—that is, "Be You; Be Yourself." "Insist on yourself; never imitate," as Emerson said, and remember what that famous author Anonymous said, "Never repress your insanity; it will drive you crazy!" And so I end with a blessing for you. I hope Diane and Karen have infected you with a bit of foolishness, because life's door fully opens to you when you remain "play-fool."

Bon "Joyage"!

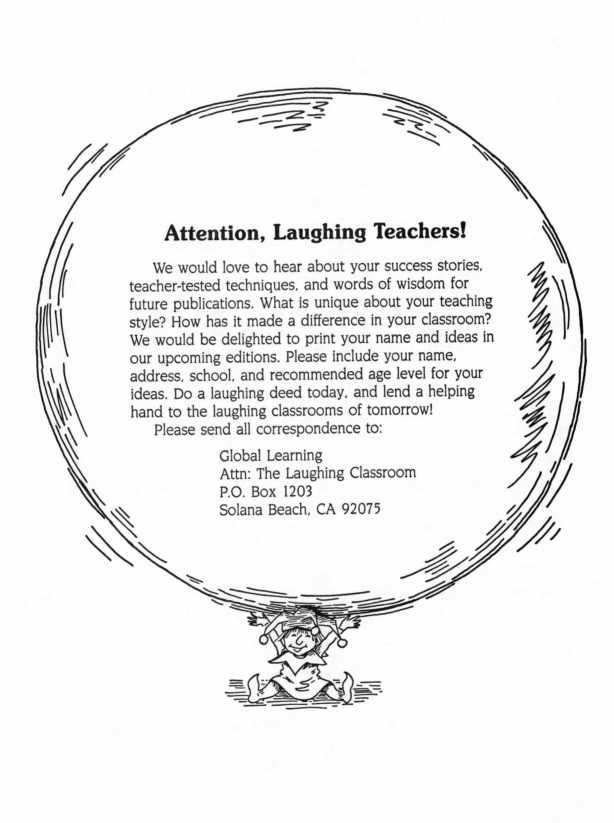

Attention, Laughing Teachers!

We would love to hear about your success stories, teacher-tested techniques, and words of wisdom for future publications. What is unique about your teaching style? How has it made a difference in your classroom? We would be delighted to print your name and ideas in our upcoming editions. Please include your name, address, school, and recommended age level for your ideas. Do a laughing deed today, and lend a helping hand to the laughing classrooms of tomorrow!

Please send all correspondence to:

Global Learning
Attn: The Laughing Classroom
P.O. Box 1203
Solana Beach, CA 92075

If you liked the book, you'll love the workshop!

The Laughing Classroom:
Effective Teaching and Discipline With Humor

From coast to coast, **Diane Looman's** dynamic program has been met with rave reviews from teachers K-12. It offers *solid content, entertaining delivery,* and *practical hands-on value.* The program includes:

- Using Warm-ups, Play Breaks, and Laughing Lessons
- Applying humor to high-risk students
- Taking discipline more seriously with humor
- Building humor into lesson planning/school curriculum

As the founder of the Laughing Classroom Workshops, Diane offers the program as a keynote speech, as a half- or full-day workshop, and as a graduate-level college course, fully accredited with several universities. Loomans is a college teacher, national speaker, and director of Global Learning; she has degrees in community education and adult education from the University of Wisconsin.

Other topics by Diane Loomans include "Self-Esteem in the 90's," "Creating a Positive Future for Our Children," "Positive Parenting," and "The Power of Laughter and Play in the Workplace." For more information or for a free catalog, contact:

Global Learning, P.O. Box 1203, Solana Beach, CA 92075
Phone and Fax: (619) 944-9842

Order Form

Please send me:

_____ copies of *The Laughing Classroom: Everyone's Guide to Teaching With Humor and Play* by Diane Loomans and Karen Kolberg @ $14.95

_____ copies of *Full Esteem Ahead* by Diane Loomans @ $14.95

_____ copies of *The Lovables in the Kingdom of Self-Esteem* by Diane Loomans @ $15.95

_____ copies of *Positively Mother Goose,* by Diane Loomans, Karen Kolberg, and Julia Loomans @ $14.95

Please enclose $2.50 shipping and handling for the first book, $1.50 for each additional book. Add tax if you are a California resident. Group discounts available!

Name_____

Address_____

City_____ State _____

Zip Code _____ Phone _____

Global Learning, P. O. Box 1203, Solana Beach, CA 92075
Phone and Fax: (619) 944-9842

Karen Kolberg has presented her unique combination of education and entertainment to corporations, educators, students, and community groups throughout the nation for the past ten years. For the past eight years, as a trainer for Playfair, Inc., Karen has led groups (from five to five thousand) in noncompetitive play experiences designed to build community, celebrate diversity, and raise serum fun levels. Drawing from her experience as a writer, actress, and director, as well as the cofounder of a national competitive improvisation company and a prevention education specialist, Karen offers time-tested techniques that can be immediately applied to any work situation, whether you're an educator, a community leader, or a student. She uses her skills as an educator, trainer, storyteller, juggler, and comedienne to make the ideas presented in *The Laughing Classroom* come to life.

Karen has developed a series of presentations entitled Celebration of Education to empower educators "to take their job seriously, but themselves lightly." (Available as keynote, seminar, or daylong workshops.)

For Students: No Brain, No Gain

Karen is both funny and informative in this keynote for kids of all ages. With a hearty dose of laughter, Karen conveys vital information about the relationship between optimism and peak performance, the mystery and majesty of the mind, and the importance of valuing oneself and others.

For Educators: I'm Laughing So Hard I Must Be Learning

Celebrate yourselves with this playful, helpful, and humorous presentation. Learn how laughter promotes higher level thinking. Analyze your personal humor style and the humor styles of your friends and colleagues. Add to your repertoire of energizers and icebreakers and share your favorite teaching techniques with your peers. You'll leave inspired, acknowledged, and brimming with ideas. This is a wonderful complementary program to Diane Loomans's Laughing Classroom Workshop.

For Corporations/Communities:
Laugher Is the Best Stress Medicine

In this upbeat keynote, Karen takes a light-hearted look at a serious subject. She looks at stress as it relates to change and homeostasis; she shows the impact laughter has on the immune system; she presents ideas about how to increase productivity by changing negative coping patterns into positive coping strategies; and she motivates and challenges the participants to take five, survive, and thrive.

For Conferences: Tap Your Funnybone

This highly entertaining, interactive keynote gets participants excited about the conference, gives them an opportunity to meet one another, and energizes them for the day. Using many of the play experiences presented in *The Laughing Classroom*, participants learn play and humor techniques by experiencing them firsthand. It's a great kickoff or wrap-up for small or large conferences.

New Playful Products From KJK Enterprises
Compliment Cards™

If you liked Fifty Ways to Say You Did Okay in Part IV: Teaching With Humor That Heals, now here's an easy and playful way to give a compliment each day. These tiny cards can be given (or hidden) to surprise and acknowledge a student or a colleague for a job well done. Feeling unappreciated? Buy a set; give them to others; ask them to acknowledge you.

Wholesale and Retail Book Orders From KJK Enterprises

Add to the levity of the planet: order one book or one hundred! Wholesale price is given by the case. Individual books are $14.95 plus shipping and handling ($2.50 first book, $1.50 each additional book).

- *The Laughing Classroom*
- *Positively Mother Goose*
- *L Is for Love* (An alphabet book for head and heart)

For booking, price, or ordering information, please call or fax (414) 276-8393, or write to:
KJK Enterprises, P.O. Box 93605, Milwaukee, WI 53203-0605